TEARS of LAUGHTER

TEARS of SADNESS

Cindy Baldwin

Published by New Generation Publishing in 2013

First Edition

www.newgeneration-publishing.com

New Generation Publishing

RETIREMENT
I'd got that covered!

With special thanks and deep gratitude to
Father Patrick Kerley whose constant and selfless
commitment to the school over many years helped
make it the success that it was.

PART ONE

BEGINNINGS!

'A word of advice Mrs Clothier, your daughter's naughtiness may be boredom. If you send her to the local school she will spend most of her time in the corridor. She and you may be happier if she goes to a small private school!'

I was four years old! Our head teacher neighbour was being helpful but my mother was horrified. I admit to crayoning on the walls of the house being built next door – my red clay handiwork standing out starkly against the white Bath limestone – but how bad was that?

As horrified as my mother was my father was delighted! They would pay for 'only the best' education they could afford.

As I looked at the upturned faces of the children in front of me 50 years later I wondered how naughty had I been?

I adored school – it was one class downstairs looked after by Miss Garroway, a dragon on first knowing but one I grew to love when I went to the class up the stairs. Up the stairs to Miss Minett's class, the owner of the school and an absolutely wonderful teacher. She didn't suffer fools gladly and knew her pupils very well, a stickler for ensuring we all did our best, and we did our best for her! Our curriculum was limited but thorough: English: I knew and understood all eight parts of speech by the time I transferred to secondary school, pointing out to my new English teacher that there were seven parts of speech, as she had said, BUT if you include the' interjection' that made it eight!! I'm not sure how I made it through the year! Maths; Shinty- a form of hockey; Country Dancing; Singing and Handicraft. I still have my felt bunny with the bloody ear where I bled over it during a nose bleed!

I learnt to read through phonic sounds and rote. Words once taught were expected to be remembered, if not I was sent to the large step down to the garden clutching the forgotten word to remember it. In practise this meant waiting for the 'Big' class upstairs to come out to play and ask one of them to tell me the word. I only forgot a few words, the humiliation of having to ask for help from a much older child made my learning of words very quick!

It worked.
By the age of ten we were group reading 'The 47 steps' by Graham Greene – who said the Literacy strategy was innovative?

I took the 11+ on a very snowy day in 1960. My father had to drive me to the other side of Bath to the school holding the exam. I was late due to the snow but by no means the latest. I remember the teacher had a lovely smile and told me not to worry; I would be given the correct amount of time and to begin when I was settled. The results arrived several months later and I remember my mother and I not understanding what a 'secondary school' meant. Did I pass or not? Was secondary a code for not gaining a Primary school place. Eventually we looked it up in the telephone book to see that the local grammar school was a secondary school. A phone call to my school head teacher confirmed our hopes that I had passed!

My first day at the 'Big' school – apart from upsetting the English teacher began well but nowadays would be thought upsetting. My father drove me to the school and let me out onto the pavement. With a kiss and a too hearty 'Have a good day' ringing in my ears I walked into the school grounds. A teacher, who insisted that I must know somebody at the school, was shepherding us into the hall where we sat on the floor until Miss Cooke, our new head teacher gave us a preliminary pep talk and we were given our class teacher's name and ushered out into our new classrooms.

One of our first needlework sessions was to learn cross stitch. Our homework was to cross stitch four letters of our surname on to a piece of given fabric. Obviously not having much imagination and seeking to complete the task to the best of my ability I used the first four letters of my surname – CLOThier. When returning our work the teacher's first words were 'Who is the clot'? We all looked round wondering who had given in such dreadful work to be called a clot. Then the dreaded piece of fabric, so lovingly worked on, was given to me! Only then did I twig what I had done BUT the good humour of my classmates made me feel that I was accepted even more as part of the group, someone who could do wrong as well as be supercilious! From that day forward I was called Clot, with great affection by all my friends.

Memories of school are numerous and mostly good. One exception being when I went out of school to buy an ice lolly from an ice cream van parked just on the roadside. No, we weren't allowed to, but my life was spent 'on the edge'! Unfortunately, a senior teacher caught me and demanded that she be given the offending lolly. More unfortunately she had on white gloves and the lolly was an ice stick that you pushed up through the plastic sleeve to eat it. The white gloved hand extended forward and took the lolly. Crimson ice and iced water gushed over on to the virgin white lace! I had a very bad afternoon that day but I never indulged in visiting the ice cream van again!

I loved school with a passion. The teachers were inspirational. I threw myself into all subjects but mostly I enjoyed the Games lessons - playing hockey and netball for the school on wet Saturday mornings was exhilarating. Though the move from first team to second team netball in upper sixth had me sobbing pathetically!

MOVING ON

My father and I decided that I would teach despite my mother's pleas that I attend a technical college to learn typing, marry a postman and live in the next street for ever!

My interview at St. Mary's Church of England Teacher Training College, Cheltenham was a bit of a 'curve ball'. I was asked what I thought about when I took the dog for a walk! I'm not sure what was wanted but I proffered answers , which seemed to be acceptable but not really what was wanted which was my creative spirit rather than the pastoral answers I gave! However, I was offered a place and in September 1966 I began a three year training course and met my roommate, and lifelong friend Sue, from Yorkshire. Sue had been practising my surname as 'Clotiey' since her arrival the day before as she thought I was French! I think my arrival was a bit of an anti climax for her. As we were laughing about this I remember my dear mother coming into the hostel with the 'obligatory' mug which I had inadvertently left in the car. She was struggling not to cry and seeing us laughing probably decided I was a very hard hearted child.

My three years zoomed past. It was a wonderful carefree life with life lived to the full both academically and socially.

I saw the new breed of students arriving to look around

in my last term. The age of majority was to change for these students from twenty one years of age to eighteen. They were so confident! No signing into their hostels before 10.00pm for them. In fact we decided we wouldn't like to be their lecturers either! Were we molly coddled?

PART TWO

STARTING OUT

My probationary teaching post was in Bilston, near Wolverhampton, at Greenacres Junior School. The first morning catapulted me into the real adult world of work!

There were two of us – both new; both probationers; both equally nervous- sitting in the empty staff room waiting to be told when to go to our new classes. Neither of us put two and two together:

- we knew where our classes were – we had been shown during the holidays –
- Staff were racing around the corridors –
- 9.00am came and went

Suddenly, like a bomb blast, **we knew**. **We** were supposed to be in a classroom; the children were in; why would anyone come and get us; **we were teachers!!** The race to our adjoining classrooms was a little unprofessional and the noise emanating from the rooms from eager new 10 year olds was startling BUT luckily no-one had noticed and our very first pupils seemed unperturbed and quite glad to have a teacher!!

It brought home to me with a jolt how 'molly coddled' I'd been at college! I realised that I had to think for myself; stand on my own two feet. I would be from now on a fully paid up member of the working society AND I was going to enjoy every minute of it!!

I thoroughly enjoyed my year at Green Acres but had met my husband to be and moved to South Tottenham in London. Teaching as a supply teacher at Pakenham St. in Brixton was a different story. BUT if you survived the first term the children did respect you and formed good relationships.

Show weakness and you were doomed!

After marrying my first husband, a journalist, we moved to Streatham where I began a three year stint at the local junior school.

CONSOLIDATION

Due to my husband's promotion to BBC producer of the early morning radio programme we moved to Norwich. I looked on the map, pleased to see that roads went all that way but it couldn't have been further from home. I was very home sick.

I placed my teaching application forms on a very large pile of other hopeful application forms at County Hall. The words ringing in my ears were

'there are few teaching vacancies and there are very many candidates. I will contact you if anything suitable comes up but do look in the newspaper for the odd advert'.

Depressed I went to 'sign on'.

Well I have never seen anything like it. I stood in one of the four queues for about two hours; I nearly got to the top of the queue when a board was put up across the glass grill, with thin steel bars, stating:

'GONE TO LUNCH BACK AT 2.00PM'

As I didn't know the area around me I stayed close to the signing on office, there were no shops nearby that I knew of so I went without lunch or coffee and waited.

The office opened on time and after what seemed like an age it was my turn. The humiliation of the whole sorry episode ensured that I didn't ever go back! However, I was given the address of HMSO at Anglia Square for the position of Casual, Casual Typing

Checker. I was never sure whether one of the 'Casual' words were misprints or whether I really was at the bottom of pile. Having said that I had a wonderful six months there. At the end of the day I still had energy to go out in the evenings; the girls were all very friendly; the office team leader was lovely to work for and if you were ever ill the work just piled up for your return – nobody told you that you should be doing it another way. The work was hard but quite rewarding and after work there was no 'homework'!

After six months I received a telephone call from a head teacher who had seen my application and wondered if I would go for an interview! I jumped at the chance and was offered, a teaching position at Wensum Junior School just as the transition from Junior to Middle schools came into force.

This was an interesting time during which, over the next few years we taught year 7 the same as we had previously taught year 6! The promise of new resources and classrooms purely for year 7, still looked on as the first year of secondary teaching in theory, proved completely incorrect. The younger children gained by using the new resources earlier in their education that they would have done previously. So year 7 just had more of year 6!

I thought standards were dropping then.....

The head master was an inspirational man in many ways and I learnt a lot from him, but he had some very strange ideas at times. He loved confrontation between staff as I found out when in my third week there I was asked to present to the staff a new English curriculum not realising the school had a co-ordinator for English!! That was interesting!

Horse riding at Holt on Wednesday afternoons! I did manage to stop him asking Princess Ann to be our sponsor and to have every child 'blooded' before they transferred to secondary school!

Annual skiing trips to Italy – we'd never have even contemplated it in my last years of headship – we would have been snowed under in paper work!

After seven exciting years I moved to Lakenham Middle school in Norwich as Upper School Co-ordinator. I spent seven years with equally questioning and interesting children.

Residential in Wales potholing – going one mile downwards with a group of six children between me and the specialist. I was given a whistle to blow if I had problems but, as we could only crawl along a very low tunnel on our tummies with miner's lamps on our heads to see the way, what would have happened if anything had gone wrong I hate to think! Then there was the swimming in deep water wearing wellies and swim gear. No health and safety then. However, it tested your own self. The children felt fear – actually we all felt fear – and we overcame our fears. It was brilliant!

Deciding I needed to move on and up I put in applications for more senior posts.

I went for an interview as a Deputy Head at a Middle school in Norwich. I felt the interview had gone extremely well; I had answered all questions clearly and coherently with personal examples and had shown my philosophy of education throughout.

However, I was flabbergasted to be told that I was the first candidate to be discarded! Apparently I had thumped the table in my enthusiasm to put over how I would support a failing teacher. Far too strong a personality!

At 37 years old, young in the 1980s to contemplate headship, but with the confidence and naivety of youth I shrugged off the disappointment and applied for the headship of Bawburgh County Primary School.

LIFE IS CIRCULAR

Ducklings covered the Broads in early 1987. The weather was hot with beautiful blue skies.

Swarms of swallows swarmed over our heads on our walks around the river. Such was the magical time of my interview.

Bawburgh School was one of many small village schools that were due for closure but saved by a change in government. The school had been kept open with a county unattached head teacher prior to my appointment but was resigned to closure. The sound of stampeding feet to the nearest middle school more central to Norwich itself was silent yet deafening.

The school was a delight to look at. Set back from a small country cul de sac lane; a simple but imposing Victorian building overlooking a field which rolled down to the River Yare. The feel as I walked through the door was one of calm and peace. A returning home to the values of my own primary school.

I can only really remember two things about the interview or rather the aftermath of the interview having been offered and accepted the position!

Firstly, the Chair of Governors explaining to me that he was terribly sorry, and that it was nothing to do with my appointment but that his child would be transferring to the middle school in September. I assured him; or rather the person who was taking my place in my body assured him that this would be fine he must make decisions for his children that he felt were the best.

The sound of now running feet grew noisier – would there be any children left?

Secondly, I, a highly organised person, just sat there whilst sherry was handed round to celebrate the new life of a school already thought of as dead. I didn't even hand round glasses I just sat there, mesmerised by what had just happened.

I returned home late with the large physical files of success under my arm. My husband swept me off my feet and took me out for a celebratory meal which, in retrospect I thoroughly enjoyed, but at the time I really needed my bed!

It was the day after my interview that I realised that I had left my 'emergency kit' at the school. I rang Pam, the secretary who had looked after us so well the previous day, who promised to keep it safe. She did admit much later on that she was amazed what she found in my carrier bag a complete kit in case things went wrong such as a cloudburst or being hit by a truck – you never know what might happen and as my mother always said 'what would the ambulance men think ...!

After my appointment I found that the teaching staff were only contracted to the school until the July and, they assured me, did not want to remain purely due to health reasons or retirement. I needed to appoint a new full member of staff immediately. In my ignorance or naivety I didn't realise what a predicament I was in until colleagues looked aghast at the challenge. I appointed Noreen Hunter, a Scottish teacher with whom I had worked at Wensum Middle School.

I moved my precious books, boxes of them, from our

attic to the school during the summer holiday. They stacked in the office ready for dismantling as time afforded.

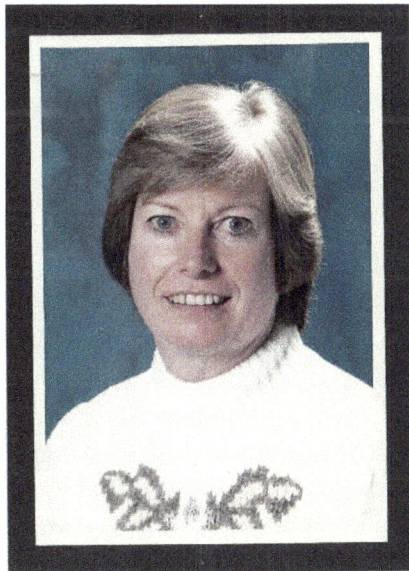

Ready for anything 1987!

PART THREE

BAWBURGH
1987 - 2008

Day one of my headship was a blinding revelation of what I didn't know and what I didn't expect!

I arrived very early and together with Noreen set out the two classrooms. I placed named cards on each two person desk and one piece of lined paper plus a brand new pencil and ruler. The work was written on the blackboard - no white boards then - in my best handwriting. I went to the office to await the secretary; answer the phone and talk to inquisitive parents. At 9.00am, the start of the school day, I went on to the playground to collect the children. Mistake number one - there were no children- apparently I learnt, at play time, that they came straight into school as they arrived. I raced to my classroom to find fewer than twenty children playing aeroplanes with my beautiful, virgin pieces of white lined paper; duelling with rulers and pencils and generally running amok! After a few minutes, during which both I and the children vied for supremacy, the children sat down. Having given out more paper and replaced broken rulers and pencils it became very apparent that the children had not been taught to use a ruler to draw a margin, in fact, they didn't know what a margin was, nor did they understand about putting the date at the top of the page or writing a heading.

By the end of the week I had admitted defeat and informed County Hall that I needed a Reception teacher for half days as Noreen and I would be splitting the Junior children into two small classes in the morning!

My load would have been lightened had my secretary arrived on that first morning but all I seemed to be doing was listing children who were arriving late. One of these was the mother of Pamela Knights who was stuck in France but, we were re-assured, that she would be with us in the morning. We couldn't even find her on the register!

No secretary meant I had no idea of how much dinner money was, nor how or who ordered or delivered it. I assumed children expecting a dinner were correct and ordered accordingly when the local Infant school rang for numbers. They informed me that the meals would arrive in thermostatically sealed boxes at approximately 11.30am. half an hour before the lunch hour began. I meticulously kept a pile of the brown envelopes with dinner money in on the office table, some obviously wanting change as notes had been sent.

When Mrs Lee, the dinner lady arrived I could have kissed her! Lunch time went according to the normal scheme of things and gave Noreen and I a chance to contemplate and re-draft our school organisation.

The end of the day couldn't have come any sooner. I wondered what stories of the new Head teacher and staff would be going home that night! Nightmares of angry parents haunted my dreams that night and the children grew extra heads hour by hour.

The next morning brought its pluses – Pamela Knights, whom we couldn't find on the registers, turned out to be Pam the secretary – aren't mothers wonderful, we are always children to them! The minuses were parents who were concerned that their children were being given work that was too hard for them, giving them a sleepless night, and that the classes were to be changed.

A huge, huge plus was meeting Mr Mrs Clements. Mrs Clements was the cleaner in charge ably supported by her husband. They were so supportive and found no problem with anything we did – even my dripping paint after a session of 'in situ' background painting of the wall boards. Anything I wanted to do was never a problem to them at all- their job was to clear up after a day's work. They wanted their village school to succeed and therefore, the more adventurous the school curriculum became, attracting more pupils, the happier they were. God bless them for that!

Those first few years were of intense excitement – pre National Curriculum and targets set rigidly from external sources; a time when the individual child could be developed, their own interests followed with no set paralysing 'units of work'! It was Noreen who brought her love of Scottish dancing to the school; we all Scottish danced with partners; we addressed the haggis annually in full Scottish dress complete with a Scottish piper!

Our curriculum emulated to some extent that of my own primary school. Maths and English were the morning sessions, ensuring that each child understood the basics of the subject. Reading was all important in the Reception class ensuring that every child could read well, use their common sense to find the necessary crayons, pencils, picture dictionaries before leaving the Reception class.

IF A CHILD IS UPSET GIVE THEM A HUG!

Surely as teachers we are primarily 'in loco parentis' and as such we are the parents of the children whilst they are in our care. Positive role models of what good parents should be like and should act.

My first school policy in 1987 was a Positive Touching policy. Get down to the child's level to talk to them, use a firm touch to console. No caresses: but a firm hug or an arm firmly round the shoulders of a child gives a bond of understanding and solidarity between you.

It's you and I against the world – When do we attack!

I am sure that part of the behavioural problems we see these days is because there is too little or no physical contact between teachers and children or indeed parents and children. We seem to have a fear of being accused of molesting children, of being accused of being a paedophile.

PRIOR TO LOCAL MANAGEMENT of SCHOOLS

A time when people had respect, and were in turn respected!
A time when people earned trust and in turn trusted each other!

Before schools were able to manage their own finances, Local Management of Schools, we were administered by the local Education authority. In our county there was a wonderfully warm man, Mr Geoff Gough, who knew all central area schools inside out. He was always ready to help whenever help was needed.

He was at the end of the phone by 7.30am any school day and I would say,

"Have you got a few minutes Geoff?"

"I'll just get my coffee" was the reply and when comfortably seated he would listen carefully to what had happened and what you were thinking of doing and then he'd say.

"Well if I was Cindy Baldwin I would be doing xxxx and xxxx".

His trademark was his tie flipped over one shoulder. His loss when he retired was felt acutely by many head teachers.

MAKING IT MINE

It soon became apparent that if I was to develop each child as an individual then I had to look at them as an individual and stop processing them through the accepted system. Some children were slower to grasp ideas but got there in the end – their self-esteem heightened – they were not stupid! However, to move these children to the next class because they were of that age seemed ridiculous to my mind because they just sank to the bottom again. In the same way a brighter child who grasped ideas quickly needed to move on to work of a higher year in order to stimulate his enthusiasm for learning.

Lack of stimulation makes children complacent or, might I say, a little 'big headed' as, at times, it did their parents also! One of our hardest jobs was to explain to a child who transferred to us from a first or infant school at the age of seven or eight was that they worked all day at Bawburgh. They consistently told us that 'after play we help the others'! Oh no not at my school, you work!

As a result our classes were based on teaching approaches rather than ages, a concept that. I feel, suits the individual better. I built up four classes:

COMETS- these were all Reception children and any year 1 or 2 who still needed that 1:1 motherly approach for whatever reason. Reading, basic mathematics and building up self esteem was the mainstay of their curriculum – lots of music, sports, art work to let them begin to understand who they were and how to use their imagination. Year 2 children who remained in Comets were identified by the school as having special educational needs and were given extra adult support and possibly put forward for a statement of Special Need which would legally guarantee additional adult help throughout their full time education.

SATELLITES – these were mostly year 2 with brighter year 1 and slower year 3 children.

ENDEAVOUR – these were mostly year 4 with brighter year 3 and slower year 5 children. Endeavour children were endeavouring to learn the skills needed in life to succeed – self presentation; taking a chance; knowing what they were good at and asking for help in those areas that they weren't good at. In other words taking charge of their own learning.

ENTERPRISE – these were mostly year 6 with brighter year 5 children. These children were learning to be entrepreneurs using the skills previously learnt and seeing how these could be used in the outside world.

Basically the whole school from year one up to year five were streamed, a system I would endorse even now for all primary schools! Parents loved the system until their child didn't move to the next class in September with their friend! Movement to the next class was flexible and many moved to the next class at the beginning of the next term or half term. Teachers were flexible in the way they taught – skills grew week by week and content knowledge was learnt by constant reinforcement of what had gone before.

However, by the time the children transferred to secondary school I can, hand on heart, say that every child had fulfilled his or her potential and were a credit to the school and their families.

There were anomalies; for instance a child who was unable to work at the same level as his peers in the next class would be moved when he or she became physically too big to remain where they were but, usually, this was a child who had been granted a statement of special need and was, therefore, provided with a teaching assistant for support in the classroom. Also the children who were bright enough academically to move on but were not socially ready stayed where they were. Self-esteem is imperative for learning and motivation, something that is always with us even as adults!

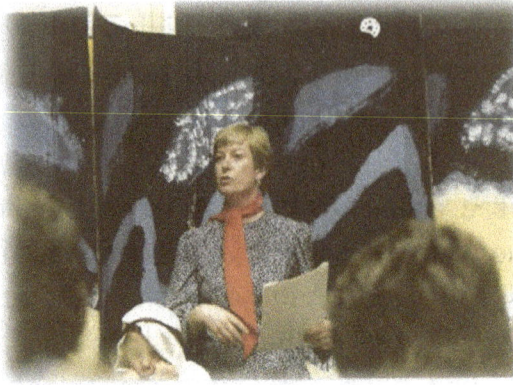

**Christmas – Talking to parents after our concert
'Meredith the Donkey' 1992**

WHAT WAS I DOING?

I had fallen into the trap of normality!
Think 'out of the box!'

It suddenly dawned on me that planning a subject for each year group when they were in the same class was counterproductive on many levels, not the least that each child was developing at their own speed regardless of age!

We taught basic Maths and English ourselves to a high level and found specialist teachers for other subjects, a pioneering concept at that time! I have always argued that unless you love a subject then you can't share a love of the subject with the children! You can teach it by using basic resources available but you can't give the children the love for the subject. A games lesson may be cancelled on many occasions if the class teacher has to take it, too cold, too hot, too windy, too many children with colds etc etc BUT a specialist games teacher arrives dressed for games, no messing! My husband can make any old piece of rock or artefact come to life as he regales why it is there, where it came from, the problems of the peoples of that time. His love of history is overwhelming whereas mine is not, due probably to history teachers who took me laboriously page by page through history text books.

I wanted my children to have a rounded education that developed all aspects of society. Not all children are academic or sporty.

AND SO:

I began to bring in specialist teachers for an afternoon a week to teach their subject throughout the school at the different levels.

I discovered a whole raft of experienced teachers who were at home feeling unable to commit to a full week or even to one or two regular days of teaching due, mostly, to having a very young family! A half day was perfect for them and by word of mouth, year on year, this wonderful wealth of experience was released!

It began with Music. I really wanted the children to be able to play an instrument and to enjoy playing music together. Singing is a wonderful way of working together and developing a sense of camaraderie with others. It gave a voice to quieter children.

We linked with a middle school in Norwich making weekly visits to learn different instruments and play together. This link also continued to develop the Personal and social side of our children. For some years we had a montage of children from both schools straddling oboes, clutching violins and playing flutes and recorders – a wonderful reminder of what can happen without the restrictions of a National Curriculum.

It was then we began Residential Weeks. Prior to mobile phones Pam and I were able to give the children different experiences of life outside of school without constant monitoring by the parents, or, alternatively, the children finding out what their parents were doing!

The environment in which learning takes place is all around us all day and needs to be seen as relevant to the child. A child learns implicitly all of the time – times in between explicit teaching gives opportunities for spiritual, moral, social and personal development.

Relevant learning is based on real life themes that are relevant to society and significant to the children. Out of school learning environments offer opportunities for the children to see and enjoy cultural diversity; community work, both voluntary and paid; develop self-esteem through sharing with others; places to eat, places to rest; forms of transport. The children become more involved in their own learning and are more able to reflect on their own progress in learning.

Our Residential trips were around North Norfolk. We used small residential hostels which took only us – negating the need to share with other schools – we had full control

FEEDBACK!

Our next foray was languages for all. French was taught throughout the school. Doors and windows were labelled 'La porte' and 'Le fenetre'! We hosted a group of teachers and educationalists from other European countries for a week highlighting our education system and , in turn, being taught different lessons by them! We learnt games and songs and cooked and ate other European foods! My children began to understand the reason for learning a language. Due to the enthusiasm of my French teacher and the success of this venture we became a recognised Comenius school.

Comenius was a group of schools obtaining grants to work in collaboration with the teachers and children in the European community. We were one of the UK schools which linked with five schools one from each of the European countries; Spain, France, Greece, West and East Germany. Each year the Head teachers and one teacher from each school would meet for three days. We discussed how the linkage was developing and how it could be further developed. The teacher representatives discussed how it was working in the classrooms and decided the topics for the next three terms. The host country changed each year and gave all my staff an opportunity to see education in other European countries, our understanding of where our own education system was in relation to others was fascinating. The annual meetings gave us a focus for the year and termly topics that each school would develop into a package of work and send duplicates to all other participating countries; we, in turn, received four packages of work on the same topic to share with our children. Much of the work was obviously pictorial and fascinating. Topics such as Family life; Games you play; Food you eat; your school day, were all exciting moments to share!

It was amazing that some countries had little or no computer technology in school. In Germany it was the local library that was so proud to let me e-mail messages to my older pupils. It was also amazing that even in the mid-1990s my children were not really interested in signing on to their e-mail account to read our missives! Looking back it took so long to 'dial up' the e-mail page and then find no messages 'got through'. Whilst Pam waited patiently, I think, in the office to re-use the phone! Now, of course, social networking demands most children have an expensive mobile phone or android to link with friends they left only ½ an hour previous. How often do we see groups of children, teenagers all on mobile phones talking animatedly to friends elsewhere? I wonder how much this practise does to the self-esteem of the parents? The husband and wife having a meal in a restaurant and a child with a mobile pressed to their ear talking to a person they couldn't let wait! We also know the problems of social texting when the intended receiver of a text unfortunately is tapped in as 'ALL' in a moment of anger or excitement and the text is sent and cannot be retrieved – ever!

I was delighted with our Language programme but within a few years I was horrified by feedback from the secondary schools which showed that my children were not taking languages as one of their options

'in fact they weren't very good at languages!'

The problem we found was that on transfer most other primary schools had not introduced a language into their curriculum and my children were repeating work previously learnt. They had become bored , mischievous and were not stimulated to take languages any further. My language teacher came up with a solution of learning a second language every other year and because of our mixed age classes a two year programme was drawn up for each language. This, together with other local schools being encouraged to teach languages at primary level helped considerably.

Spurred on from our interest and success with other European schools we became an International School in 1996. This was a very exciting year.

Life was good!

But more of that later!

EASTERN DAILY PRESS

Norwich, is making a name for itself with a series a national awards and an ethos 'citizenship and getting to know yourself', which is spurring excellent results.

The Bawburgh School has earned a fine reputation as an outstanding primary school.

In 1996, they were awarded the Investor in People status, 1999 finalists in the East of England's Excellence Awards and Headteacher, Cindy Baldwin, was a finalist in the leadership section of the TSB Teaching Awards.

"We are a small, rural school where individuals count," said Mrs Baldwin.

"Our ethos is based on moral Christian standards, as a result the children are well disciplined and well motivated. The atmosphere here is very good, everyone knows eachother and the children are geared to learning.

"We place a high emphasis on the future, and we encourage pupils to explore foreign cultures to understand the world we live in."

Indeed, this is emphasised by their involvement in the Comenius Project, a joint initiative between the school and various European countries including Spain, Germany, Holland and Greece. The idea is for local youngsters to understand, through exchange of work and teachers, about the similarities and differences between European nations. Pupils exchange regular e-mails discussing life in their country and send projects to one another so an understanding of different cultures can be obtained. Beyond this, they have developed their work to include other places including Eygpt, Sweden, Austria and South America.

Closer to home Bawburgh School has forged a close relationship with neighbouring Easton Col-

Pride is a word synonymous with Bawburgh School

lege. Students as an integral part of the Country Management Scheme, teach children about the countryside, wildlife and preservation.

Observing an Inch Worm, pupil, 11 year old Harvey Palgrave said, "I really enjoy looking at insects, it's interesting to learn about them and sometimes you forget how many different living things can be found in a garden."

With the support from the Friends of Bawburgh School, who have helped finance an extension, adventure play ground and various pieces of equipment, the school, it's staff and pupils are looking forward to what the 21st Century holds. The take-away diner service is already proving popular and provides a first class service to people in the local area.

43

SOCIETY CHANGES FOR THE BETTER?

In the late 1980's early 1990's a change began to permeate our school life. Marriages were beginning to break up more quickly and a 'new daddy' became a more open discussion on the playground. Children no longer kept 'home secrets' to themselves. Telling home truths so openly at Carpet Time in the Reception class extended throughout the school, even to the older children.

Now children who had already experienced Mums and Dads parting were talking to children new to the idea. I'd like to say that they were trying to help, indeed many were, but there were the few who used these difficult times to score points, almost a 'now you're the same as us' attitude!

It was always the man who left home leaving Mum to pick up the pieces of the children's lives and to keep the school run going as well as everything else. Primary schools do tend to be dominated by women, both teachers and teaching assistants, and ours was no exception. We used to take male teacher trainees but they used to leave at the end of their 6 week teaching practice, again compounding the view of some children that men were untrustworthy and unable or unwilling to commit to anything.

One of our school's strengths was its support of parents and the help we gave to family relationships. Many of the Mums were new to parenthood; being a separated Mum was even harder to accept. It was the oldest child who found it very hard to adapt to a new place in society; a place that earlier in their short lives they had been led to believe was unacceptable, being a member of a single parent family.

Was this a lesser place in society?

A place where your friends could no longer be your friends because other parents were afraid of – of what?

Were they keeping their husbands safe?

Did they feel the newly separated mother would try and befriend other husbands?

BACK TO YOUR ROOTS!

I firmly believe that everyone returns to their roots eventually. In the same way that I believe that you are what you are when you are born. From my experience, the change in behaviour of a child who dislikes change, for example being with a new teacher or transferring to a new year group manifests itself in many ways. Some will show aggression others total docility. This can be seen at an early age and such a child will always dislike or be uncomfortable with changes in their lives. BUT by understanding themselves and understanding why they re-act in this way and acknowledging that this is the way they are leads to the development of life skills, coping strategies on which to build future changes in their lives constructively and, though not without worry, with a positive attitude that if they put these strategies into place they will come through!

My roots were of a small primary school which was not a church school but held faith as its centrepiece. Belief in God helped us through our daily lives; we worked hard; we played hard, but always fairly and with mutual respect, accepting differences between us and helping each other through thick and thin. Telling lies was an absolute taboo.

The ethos of the school was of fun ' pre health and safety' – when I climbed a small tree with a rope I came down but hit my knees on the wall the tree grew against. Did I get any sympathy? NO! I just flabbergasted everyone by not putting my feet out to stop myself hitting the wall. It was a lesson learnt!

The teachers knew each of us very well – we were part of a team to equip each of us for moving into the world ahead. Life skills were of the essence each day. It was my Head teacher of that school that I turned to in years to come for an independent point of view.

This was what I wanted for my school and for my children.

SOCIETY CHANGES FOR THE WORSE?

At this time, 1990's, many of our children transferred to Wymondham High School. I wanted a link with the school that I could embed into our school culture prior to our children's transfer, something or some organisation that they could trust for the future. Teachers come and go, parents come and go but, at that time the church was steadfast in its teachings and I felt would always be there for my children.

I had begun to worship at Wymondham Abbey and on my first visit I met Reverend Father Patrick Kerley. He delivered the sermon on that day on the subject of 'being alone in the wilderness and looking for direction', just the person who would have empathy with my children should they become 'lost' in later life. After a few weeks I asked if he would come to school and talk to the older children about the strength of prayer. The link lasted for 15 years until my retirement.

From the moment of his first visit 'I' became 'We' and 'My School' became 'Our School'.

Father Patrick

Father Patrick was physically big with an equally big presence. His faith shone through him in all he said and did. The children loved him and his 'devil may care' attitude to life. "Go for it" he'd say,

"God will be there to help you but maybe not as you
expected him to be.
God will answer your prayers but not as you had
perhaps hoped!
God has a plan for all of us if we trust in him and let
him lead our lives"

Some mums, however, found it hard to see their sons putting such a value on another man. But such was the fun we had during his work with us that eventually, even the most hardened Mums, were won over by the enthusiasm their children showed in the extra 'bits' we were able to include into the year's work.

FP, as he was endearingly called by staff, became a School Governor and eventually the Chair of Governors, a position he held for many years.

A GOOD CHAIR OF GOVERNORS IS YOUR 'CRITICAL FRIEND'!?

"It's a walk in resource cupboard!" I said emphatically to F.P. but with a certain amount of pride.

"Take off the doors and use the walk in space as an extension to the office."
"BUT it's a WALK IN CUPBOARD!!" my voice rose, perhaps a little too shrilly, as I shuddered at the sacrilege of such an action.

"But it's a waste of valuable space! What do you do in that space?"
"We stand in it because it's a walk in cupboard!" I felt I was stating the obvious.

Gradually, drip by weekly drip I began to see the point. A walk in cupboard was a thing to be cherished but perhaps it was a waste of space.

Months later, with doors removed and repositioned one metre in, we had a larger, more effective office and a good sized resource cupboard, exactly the same size as it was before!

STRIVING FOR THE BEST

1996 was both a culmination of our work and the basis on which our future work was based.

Just before the end of the Christmas term an Ofsted inspection, specifically looking at our decision to employ part time subject specialist teachers, awarded us the grade of 'Outstanding'.

Then things took off!

We were asked to meet the education minister in London together with two hundred other progressive head teachers. We came from all over the country; all awarded Outstanding by an Ofsted team and more importantly we were all working 'out of the box', all in different ways but all of them in an entrepreneurial way which involved our children engaging in the real world, teaching outside of the classroom.

The conference was the brain child of Prince Charles and the Chief Inspector of Schools, Chris Woodhead: both being dedicated to schools thinking in new ways to capture the children's interest and determination to succeed.

This meeting led to us being asked to become involved in supporting a National teacher training programme for mature students based at Nottingham University. We were one of only forty seven schools in the UK to be part of the Nationally Outstanding School Centred

Initial Teacher Training programme, OSCITT. The only downside was that our nearest partner school was in Milton Keynes or Nottingham. Not too good for the termly area meetings! However, you can do a lot of work on the train provided you have a fully charged lap top!

School wins Prince's praise for training role

The Prince of Wales has given his seal of approval to a Norfolk primary school.

The Prince has written to Bawburgh County Primary congratulating it on becoming one of the first to join the National Consortium of Teacher Training Primary Schools.

Classified as "outstanding", the edge-of-Norwich school is one of only 47 selected to take on postgraduate student teacher training throughout the year.

The scheme is applauded by Prince Charles, who has written to all schools in the initiative.

"I should like to offer my thanks and congratulation to the headteachers of the schools, who have achieved so much and will, I am sure, continue to play their vital role in the drive to raise educational standards and rediscover the true purpose of education," he writes.

A delighted Cindy Baldwin, head of Bawburgh Primary, said: "It's a real tonic to have our work recognised and singled out."

MINIBUSES - THE WAY TO EDUCATION IN THE WORKING ENVIRONMENT!

I wanted our children to see what the real world was like and to see the reason for learning.

Coaches were prohibitively expensive and parents were being asked for a good deal of money for each outing.

Children whose parents couldn't afford the trip were paid for out of school funds - it was imperative that no one was left out of the exciting outside learning environment.

We decided to look into purchasing our own minibus!

Wow, they were expensive. However, we had an exceptionally supportive PTA who having raised funds for the new classroom needed a new goal. Actually they had lots of goals but this one was top of the list. Over three years, through a range of fund raising events, they had raised enough for our first minibus!

The cheers as we drove it onto the playground with the whole school on the playground were deafening!

We blessed the new minibus during our assembly outside on the playground. It was now part of our family and gave us a new sense of freedom. A freedom to take our children wherever we needed to in order to expand their horizons!

We had often borrowed other schools' minibuses and

were a little horrified by the state they were in. We put this down to the fact that most staff could drive the minibuses. At that time there was no county minibus training. We put it to governors that we should have two named drivers only. Something the Governors were in complete agreement over.

It was felt that I should be one named driver as I did not have a full time teaching commitment. Father Patrick should be the second named driver as he also had no teaching commitment and would probably be freer to drive.

The beauty with this arrangement was no teaching staff would be taken out of the classroom if someone needed a driver for a school trip.

When it came into being we both took the County Minibus driving course and passed.

Two named drivers was an issue with staff wanting to take children out when both drivers were busy. I felt that perhaps I should listen and we did try and train a third person as a named driver. But on the first outing, with no children on board, despite assurances that the person had driven a large power steering motor before, the side of the minibus was taken off getting onto the road. The decision to have three named drivers was reversed!

Before I retired the governors were able to use part of the money they had invested in a high rate deposit account to buy a new second minibus. The two minibuses enabled us to take a whole class out at the same time – a wonderful resource to develop our learning in the 'Real World'.

Royal praise for 'basics' school head

By DAVID MACAULAY
Public Affairs
Correspondent

The Prince of Wales was so impressed with the back-to-basics teaching methods of a Norfolk school that he has invited its head to an audience at Highgrove.

Cindy Baldwin of Bawburgh Primary is believed to be the only Norfolk headteacher to be invited to the reception on July 16, courtesy of teaching methods which put emphasis on Christian values.

The Chief Inspector of Schools, Chris Woodhead, who made a trip to the school this year, has put it forward as a base for teacher training under his School Centred Initiative for Teacher Training (SCITT).

School-centred teacher training is at the heart of a political row with Don Foster, the Liberal Democrats' education spokesman, who claims Mr Woodhead is acting "in cahoots" with the Prince

IMPRESSED: The Prince of Wales

of Wales to promote an initiative in conflict with government policy.

The Prince's private secretary, Stephen Lamport, wrote in a letter to Bawburgh School that his employer had invited heads "in order to give his support and encouragement to schools which reflect a particularly high standard of teaching."

He added: "His Royal Highness wishes very much to recognise the importance of

schools which provide an effective grounding in the basic skills needed by our children, and which are an example to others of the best in our primary school system."

Mrs Baldwin sympathises with the Prince's recently aired attack on "trendy" teaching methods developed in the 1960s.

Putting the case for more traditional methods yesterday, she asked: "There was a philosophy that children should only read when they are ready to do so and want to, but who will want to learn to read?"

She said the school was unorthodox because of its strong emphasis on Christian values and a large number of teachers who specialise in subjects. "We have a very good Christian ethos which I believe has fostered a caring atmosphere," she added.

Mrs Baldwin said the visit was a follow up to a London conference she was invited to by Mr Woodhead in May.

57

CHRIS WOODHEAD CAME TO SEE OUR SPECIALIST TEACHING IN ACTION

Chris Woodhead made the long journey to visit the school to talk with both the children but also the specialist teachers. The morning went very well and he was very interested in what the teachers had to say.

He spoke to many of the children about their work and how they were taught. He was keen to see whether they liked lots of different teachers or would prefer just the one class teacher. The older children were at pains to tell him that this was an advantage for transferring to secondary school because they would be used to a different teacher per subject!

He was also intrigued by the 'Homework Books'.

Due to some of the subject teachers only coming in on one day a week they set the homework but couldn't take it in until the next week. So we devised a homework book based on secondary school ideas which showed parents the day on which the work was to be handed in. Parents could then help their children decide on which night to complete the homework. It showed children who left homework till the last minute that they might have to complete two or three bits on one night! These books helped children to think for themselves and to plan their own work at home.

Feedback from children who had transferred to secondary school said that this had helped them enormously because they were used to the system.

Mr. Woodhead seemed excited by what he had seen.

He asked for sandwiches to eat in the car on his return journey rather than a hot meal at the school. Rather embarrassingly we did not realise that he was bringing a colleague with him – the sandwiches which he said he would prefer to our hot meal, to eat on the journey home, were wholly inadequate for two people! I felt his memories of us would reflect our diminished meal. But NO an e-mail sent October 2010 to support us stated:

> *'I do remember our visit to your school - it*
> *stays in my mind as one of the best*
> *primary schools I saw whilst I was*
> *Chief Inspector.'*

by SIMON WRIGHT

A PRIMARY school near Norwich has been hailed as a blueprint for the future by one of the Government's top education advisers.

Chief Inspector of Schools Chris Woodhead toured Bawburgh Primary yesterday to see a system based on part-time specialist teachers in action.

The school has just four full-time teachers.

Seven visiting specialist teachers take lessons including science, art and geography.

It is a system Mr Woodhead believes is the way forward and, after talking to head Cindy Baldwin, staff and children, he proclaimed it a success.

"This is a very interesting and exciting primary school and I have been deeply impressed with the leadership and quality of teaching," he said.

"They use specialist teachers which doesn't happen in many primary schools and I was intrigued to see how successful it was in practice.

"The specialists help the permanent teachers deal with the broad range of subjects that the national curriculum requires. And the children benefit from visiting teachers with particular expertise and enthusiasm."

Mr Woodhead added: "I knew it was happening in some schools but until today I had not visited a school where it was happening to this extent.

"I don't see why it can't be done elsewhere and I think there are lessons which could be learned from this school in Norfolk and beyond."

► More on Mr Woodhead's visit on page 18.

GOING IT ALONE

It was Geoff Gough who asked for a list of all schools nationwide who were called to the meeting in London. He seemed to feel that our county should develop these links to see if it could lead the way with some more entrepreneurial leadership in schools.

Although he, himself, felt the way ahead was a different place it was not followed through. What happened to the list I have no idea. However, I do know that from the setting up of the Nationally Outstanding SCITT programme schools in the group changed dramatically for the better.

Different counties administer things in a different way. Some are more positive and entrepreneurial in approach than others. It was fascinating to visit other schools in other counties to see how things were done differently.

In one county all children had hot school dinners apart from the 20 or so who could bring a packed lunch as that was the most the school could put in their fridge to keep them cool! I can see why this wasn't very popular with parents but that was the school rules, backed by the county education department. However, when I asked if we could do this there was no support and we weren't allowed to go forward with this initiative.

The other schools earned thousands of pounds through the sale of school lunches and were able to build better teaching facilities. The provision of class resources, building of staff rooms and better parking facilities was something I saw year on year at meetings and of which I was very envious. But 'not to be in our county'! No wonder then that we looked outside our county for In Service Training for our teaching and non-teaching staff!

CAUGHT UP - NOW WHAT?

Things had been going so fast we could hardly keep up but then everything stopped and I felt moribund! On a train back from Milton Keynes I put on paper how I felt.

MY MIND

Like dishwater
Innovative ideas swim on the peripheral
Creating a colourful web of large objects
Colour
Vital, stimulating interaction of children's groups
Playing
Smiling
Vibrant with imaginative chatter
Noise
How?
When?
Stagnant!
Complacent!
Move!
Become involved
Work
Re-build your mind
Do!
Build!
Buy!
Discover
Breathe easy!

Where was God in all of our work?

God has always been with me in my life. Don't get me wrong I didn't initially invite him to be there but I knew he was there.

When I was about five or six years old I watched as the 'big' boys walked their bicycles up a 1:3 hill at the end of our road and then rode down, skidding round the sharp left hand turn at the bottom. How far up the hill each one went depended on how courageous they felt! It was a very organised piece of work:

One person was needed at the bottom of the hill to signal all was clear; one person waited at the bottom of the hill on the opposite side of the road to stop any riders going over the hill at the bottom, a drop of about twelve to fifteen feet to the road below. Iron railings had been positioned to stop anyone falling over onto the hill below but due to subsidence these were only a few inches above the ground, no help at all. I had a three wheeler blue bike with a boot at the back and looked longingly at the game. However, the boys would not let me have a go until I was older with a two wheeled bike. Those were the days when playing outside in the road, a cul de sac in this case, was safe and everyone looked after and protected each other. However, the boys tended to go home for tea about 4.00 o'clock and one day I had an idea. Actually I had had the same idea for many days but getting my courage up to do it took a little longer. The day in question emerged. I waited quietly until everyone had gone and then pushed and struggled to get my three wheeler up the hill – only a little way, just enough - I looked around. It looked a long way down to me but when I turned my bike around I could hardly hold it back. There was no way I could get it back down safely. There was no answer to this except, get on the bike and go down. I kept my feet off the pedals because I knew they would go too fast for my legs to keep up and my toes would hit the floor, pulling my foot underneath the bike and disaster. So I climbed on and let my sorely stretched fingers off the brakes. Wow I was off! Although I was going really fast, the wind making my eyes smart, in my head it was in slow motion. I was pointed directly down the hill towards the railings and certain death or at least a very bad crash. The newspaper headlines were illuminated clearly in my head,

"Girl dies falling over railings to the road below".

Then the most wonderful thing happened.

My bike was steered or rather pulled round the corner of the road into a telegraph pole and I fell off! My boot was buckled - how? I was shocked but unhurt! Nobody was around! Years later I still look at that telegraph pole. It is about ten yards away from the corner - how did I get there?

I knew then that God was with me and would always be there.

As I grew older I forgot him and went my own way. I remember living in London and being absolutely terrified by tremendous winds that used to sway the block of flats in which I lived. I was so insulated from the natural world that anything I couldn't control was terrifying.

Living in Norfolk I love the wind and storms that man

cannot control. The excitement of watching and feeling God's world, the one he created, the one we are all living in whether we like it or not!

We had noticed that when things were going well in school then something happened to stop us in our tracks. Our faith kept us going but we had some real knocks! The adviser who didn't like how we were organising the classes; the parent who didn't want the crucifixion mentioned at Easter; the parents who didn't want the Residential Week to be so far away; the parents who told us that we had 'done' the story of Mary and Joseph last year and could we do a different Christmas story etc etc

God provides if asked but possibly not as expected: even I didn't expect things to happen so quickly!

IT HAD BEEN A REST - NOW WE WERE OFF AGAIN"

Our World of Work programme suddenly came into its own!
We had always had a World of Work ethos which went across all age groups and was split into four areas:

The youngest children learnt about people who worked in our school and the jobs we did. They interviewed us and seemed surprised at the different things we did. Can you imagine how surprised they were to find out that the head teacher cleaned the toilets when the caretaker was ill!

Satellites learnt about the people who worked and brought things to the school. The postman; lunch deliverer; builders; FP; meter readers. All interviewed and their job specifications scrutinised, especially by the boys who wanted to know a lot about the electrical items used and the vans!

Endeavour went out into the local community to see what work was in the local area. They were taken around Roys, a local supermarket, and later Sainsbury's to see how products were marketed and what jobs were needed to run a supermarket. A little too early for the 'BOGOF' era but similar incentives were running even then.

It was very sad in the later days of my headship to hear

elderly people say that they were 'frightened' to talk to children in case they were thought of as paedophiles. They loved being interviewed because children asking them something made them feel safe to talk to them.
What a world we are developing!
Our children just loved talking to people and were so polite!

The oldest class, Enterprise, went further afield to Norfolk businesses. It became part of our Work Experience week with FP and Lorna because of one question!

"WHAT DO YOU DO ON THE OTHER SIX DAYS OF THE WEEK IF YOU ONLY WORK ON SUNDAYS?"

This question from a year 6 child was the catalyst of our World of Work programme for the oldest Enterprise children.

We were already thinking of how we could widen the children's ideas of work and this question showed their naivety on two levels:

- firstly, what did they think Father Patrick was doing on Wednesdays when he taught them RE and
- secondly it showed a lack of understanding of the implicit commitments there were in the workplace!

'World of Work' week was only for year 6 children and it was to let the children experience the differences between working environments; voluntary and paid work; time commitments.

"I want to work in an office!"

was a constant wish but when shown a single person in an office the cry became

"No not like that, more people!"

However, a visit to an open plan police headquarters office changed the cry to

"Not that many, just a few!".

The experience allowed each child to understand more what their personal needs were.

It was the same when Father Patrick showed them his study in his house and what he had to do during the week. Lorna, his wife, completed housework around him; the call of the TV was only in the other room, people just came into the garden without knocking – 'well this is a church house isn't it!'

FATHER PATRICK IN 'PLAY CLOTHES'

The children began to realise the self-control needed to work from home, some loved it. Others felt they wouldn't be able to ignore the call of snacks or TV and this environment wasn't for them!

The children shared examples of FP's work.

They helped Lorna make scones for the staff meeting and circulated with the staff afterwards; they put up a marquee ready for the summer fete in the garden; they met with the Sunshine club, an over 60's club and entertained them with some of our songs before joining in with a session of Bingo; they met the church warden who showed them round the church; they met parishioners; they took holy communion to the sick in their homes and they began to understand the intricacies of making your own timetable when things change from week to week.

At Great Yarmouth FP let us accompany him when taking Holy Communion to the sick; he taught us the ritual of not talking whilst the wine and bread was in the minibus with us as a matter of respect.

The children visited as many types of business as we could manage. The packing factory at Great Yarmouth gave them the opportunity to see workers who worked in one area only for set times each day. Trolley breaks bringing in hot tea and cakes or sandwiches was the only break in the work routine. It was surprising how many children found that good for them. They didn't want the responsibility of having to plan their own time, they wanted it planned for them.

A visit to Jarys' funeral parlour in Yarmouth was an annual must. I know it sounds awful but, firstly we saw no bodies. Some children were relieved and some not so at this information.

On our first visit we watched as a man was coming to terms with an apple computer. It was tiny in comparison to today's PCs but was, at that time 'state of the art'. He was making words for headstones by printing a computer generated stencil from a lithograph. The picture was printed onto a thin lino which, when the stencil bits were pulled of, was sticky on one side. This had been printed to exactly the correct size for the headstone and when all the stencilled bits were pulled of the lino was placed onto the headstone and stuck down firmly showing the stone only through the stencilled pieces. The stone was then put into a sand blaster and blasted for about five minutes. When the stone came out the lithograph was removed and the words had been cut into the headstone only needing gold leaf to be brushed onto the words to produce a beautiful headstone but costing a fraction of the cost of a stone chiselled headstone.

The children were able to help the man to familiarise himself with his new Apple computer, luckily we had one at school. But also I pointed out to the children the man had a disc with only three pictures – a rose, a car and a horse. There was an opportunity for an entrepreneur to produce a disc with lots of other pictures ready for funeral parlours. The following year there were so many discs with so many pictures it was unbelievable. Enterprise at work!

Coffins of different woods; shrouds of different colours with matching cushions!
It's no good saying 'I want to be buried in a cream shroud if nobody knows. Make sure it's in your will!'

By the end of the visit the reverence given to the dead person and how the coffins were made so individually enabled the children re-think death. It was something we will all do but our bodies will be looked after according to our wishes IF we tell people what we want. Making a will was another business and could be done whenever once they had started working.

When Lorna and FP moved to Eyke in Suffolk our visits were extended.

The police helicopter which was based in Suffolk had apparatus on board which could look into your garden from its pad in Suffolk! The children were amazed to see their house and outbuildings.
It was the girls who loved the helicopter: they loved sitting in it with large headphones on and map reading for the pilot. Pilots, map readers, police all combined in one job.

The Lifeboat based at Aldburgh was also interesting because again there were jobs to be done, a shop to be run to bring in funds for the boat. However, all but one of the crew were volunteers and worked in local shops with a pager on their belt. This showed the children commitment to a job which didn't pay. They were fully absorbed in the short film they were shown depicting rescues with which the lifeboat had been involved.

The boat was enormous; the place where people rescued sat was tiny; the bits of electrical equipment staggering. Trying on the clothes, socks in boots all ready to dive into, gave them a sense of the urgency of a rescue.

It was tenable; something they could all do when they were a bit older!

We tried to keep a video diary of all we did

Work experience week was just that, work times! We left school at 7.30 - 8.00am each morning to travel to Father Patrick's parish. The first few years this was only fifteen miles, a return journey of thirty miles a day. However, in the latter years a change of parish was a round trip of one hundred and twenty miles!

"Father Patrick and Lorna do this every week for us" I'd say.

"We've only got to do it for five days!"

The disruption to family life this caused was awarded with a BBQ for all families at the rectory on the Friday. An event that the children catered for by purchasing the food from the local markets and bidding for the chickens at the local livestock market! This in itself was quite an experience!

A certificate was presented to all children and their families who had managed the whole week – no days off - during the following week's assembly!

Peter Smith and family have Conquered Work Experience Week 2007. Congratulations!

This emblazoned on a photograph of the child doing something during the week gave it special significance.

The three of us having a well-earned break

In 2000 The Lord Chamberlain was 'commanded by Her Majesty' to invite Father Patrick and I to the Queen's Garden Party held at Buckingham Palace on 20th July for our 'Services to Education'. It was a wonderful day which we will always remember.

**The Queen's Garden Party –
Outside Buckingham Palace July
20th 2000**

NO NEED TO ASK FOR MONEY!

Whatever we needed seemed to be found for us in a variety of ways. The Friends of The Bawburgh School were fantastic at fund raising, especially if they knew that there was something special we wanted.

The extra classroom.
The minibus
White boards
Demolition of a wall to make my classroom larger

Grants became available

In 2002 an unsolicited letter arrived from the local nursery. The nursery was an extension of a nearby nursery which was full to overflowing and had only just relocated to our village. This hadn't proved to be successful and the nursery was apparently in financial difficulties, so much so that it was in imminent danger of closure unless a new owner could be found who would refinance!

At that time the school governors did not want the responsibility of taking over a nursery as a private venture and there was no support from the County authorities for the nursery becoming an NCC nursery.

After a good deal of thought Father Patrick and I felt that owning a private nursery ourselves was a possibility. When I say 'felt' I mean FP decided over the weekend that we could do this ourselves if we could increase nursery pupil numbers to make it financially viable. It did seem a godsend to the school for a variety of reasons the most important being that children whose parents wished them to transfer to the school would have already had the grounding necessary for our reception year. We would be able to offer education from 2 years old to 11, and if we could develop our links with the secondary school education from 2 – 18 years!! The rub being the refinancing!

After much discussion we each decided to put £5,000 of our own money into the nursery to ensure staff were paid and essential equipment bought. As this was a long term project we acknowledged that recouping our money might take many years but the excitement and importance of the venture won through.

The importance of 'Good' nursery education was imperative for all children. It would be an exciting venture that we could develop once I retired. It also meant that the transfer from the Nursery to the school would be seamless with shared learning experiences in the last years of Nursery.

The nursery was registered with Ofsted and NCC as a private nursery under the name 'The Bawburgh School Nursery'. Although its address was the Village Hall our mail address was the school as it was more convenient for me to receive mail at the school. The registered address was my home.

Although parents were made very aware in our brochure that a place at the nursery did not guarantee a place at the school, as NCC transfer rules applied, it did ensure that the school always had a full reception intake every year.

Although this was excellent I could foresee a time when the school building would physically be too small for our growing community. Our financial budgeting was based on small business principles in the real world not just school based practices. We followed the rigors of the British Quality Foundation standards. We were, therefore, delighted to be in the finals of the East of England Business Excellence awards three years in a row, in the company of other businesses . However, winning in the third year proved that our finance strategy was fully embedded into the school ethos - 'Best value for money' - only the very best for the children whether it be in equipment, training or personnel!

Following Marconi Systems, the previous year's winner was a tribute to our successful business model

Norwich Advertiser Tel: 01603 740222   www.advertiser-online.co.uk

News

Excellence award for local school

BAWBURGH SCHOOL head teacher Cindy Baldwin was in a jubilant mood last Wednesday night after fighting off stiff competition from local businesses to scoop the East of England Excellence Award.

Hosted at Dunston Hall by Stewart White, of BBC's Look East, the Awards Dinner was a celebration of organisations in the East of England who have managed to achieved high levels of excellence.

This was the third year running that the school had been shortlisted for an award.

Last year it scooped a special commendation for the school's contiguous improvement, but this year proved to belong to Mrs Baldwin, school governors and her staff.

Mrs Baldwin said: "When it was announced that we had won, I felt absolutely tremendous, I was delighted for the team, we have worked so hard to achieve such high standards.

"Now everything is embedded in the culture in the school we can move even further forward. Our school is poised to grow in strength on a secure footing."

The East of England Excel-

lence Awards recognise businesses who have managed to achieve a high standard of excellence.

This is based on the 'European Foundation for Quality Management Business Excellence Model'.

Cindy Baldwin receives her award from last year's winner Alex Hannam, managing director of Alenia Marconi Systems, and host, BBC's Look East presenter, Stewart White.
Picture: Audio Visual Unit Ltd

PLAYING FIELD
V
HALL AND PLAYING FIELD?

I had always been aware that as the school grew there would come a time when the space around us would be insufficient for all children who wanted to come to us. I had eyed up the field behind the school as a possibility for more space but there didn't seem to be any possibility......

Then I espied in the local paper:

House for sale + xx acres of agricultural land
Bawburgh

As the land was agricultural land it couldn't be used for building BUT it was adjacent to our playing field which was in the permitted building pocket. In fact one or two very large houses had already been built at the end of our road priced in the region of £500,000.

Our playing field was prime building land!

Kerching!

We had the full support of the governing body to sell our playing field and buy the much larger field at the back as our new playing field. The financial implications were potentially enormous. There would be money to build a hall, a much needed kitchen and more! It seemed such a simple answer to our difficult problem of space. Little did any of us realise at the time how long proceedings were to take or the twists and turns and complexities of the chase.

***

We had come so close to having a hall built before. Early in the 1990s the governors were sent plans drawn up by NCC and had made several changes to the window sizes. All was well. As we were the largest school in Norwich not to have a hall there was only one the final meeting to sign the agreement to the build.

What could go wrong?

I slept soundly that night dreaming of hall furniture and PE equipment.

The call the following morning was devastating – at the meeting the area was changed from Norwich to Norfolk and there was no way we were the largest Norfolk school without a hall.

***

I rang County Hall and unfolded the plan, sell our prime building land with a million pound potential and buy the cheaper agricultural land earmarking the profit to provide the school with a hall and a professional community size kitchen. I was flabbergasted to be told that NCC could not be seen to be making money on such a deal and could not make the first move. However, I could make the first move and then NCC could take over. The all-important phone call was made to the estate agents who were duly interested if a little perplexed that although I had rung further negotiations would be with NCC.

However, it was three years before the school opened the new hall and kitchen. What with the land being taken off the market and then put on again and NCC getting cold feet about the viability of the scheme the simple scheme seemed doomed.

Then permission was granted with a few alterations. The money from the sale which was originally ring fenced for the school gradually became NCC money but they would be paying for the new hall and the kitchen. Money left in the pot, with which we had hoped to keep as a safety net with which to reroof the school and purchase a new boiler as necessary did not materialise.

However, all was good to go! We had the designated builder, a local firm with good connections to the school, we just needed a start date!

I had a phone call to attend a meeting at County Hall with the then Deputy Director of Education, without whose support we would never have got this far, and for whom I have a great admiration for her honesty and tenacity.

I wasn't unduly worried about the meeting but was stunned by the sight of salmon sandwiches and a lady from finance. Not that the lady from finance always came bearing salmon sandwiches but we were never fed when we went to meetings at county hall, not meetings like this, on our own!

I was told gently but emphatically that a building of this size and expense could only be built by one of five Norfolk builders. They were excellent builders I am sure but they were also the most expensive!

What exactly is a cartel?

My protestations that NCC already knew of our builder and had not objected held no ground. It was a 'fait accompli'

I came away hungry, the sandwiches lost their charm after the second sentence, clutching a list of the five builders from which the governors were to choose their builder.

The phone call to our local builder was heart breaking; he had been involved all along; it would have been a real coup for his firm. He felt the unfairness as much as I did. I don't think his father ever really understood or forgave me.

CAROLS NEVER WERE THE SAME AGAIN – EVER!

My wonderful secretary's spelling was normally perfect. However, one year – possibly a busier than usual year – it was extremely difficult to maintain our usual professional selves during our Christmas Carol Service as verses with slight misnomers appeared during our singing.

The obviously nuclear beans!

Silent night, holy night!
Son of God love's pure light.
Radiant beans from Thy holy face
With dawn of redeeming grace,
Jesus Lord, at Thy birth.
Jesus Lord, at Thy birth.

Perhaps her thoughts had strayed to a Christmas present for herself!

Thus spake the seraph,
And forthwith
Appeared a shining thong
Of angels praising God, who thus
Addressed their joyful song
Addressed their joyful song

It only needed the two out of seven carols to have mistypes but it kept us going for years even when the carols had been typed with perfection!

LINKING SCHOOL AND THE WORLD

Many children are not academic and feel undervalued and failures in the present system. Schools are judged on academic success; a certain percentage of a set age group gaining a given standard.

When I was at school we were taught that average meant most, with some not achieving average, and some gaining more than most. A perfect parabola! The average number of black jacks in a bag for 1 penny was four but a few had three and some had five!! The National curriculum expectation for 11 year old primary children when Standardised Assessment Tests (SATs) began was for the average child to gain a level 4, some level 3 and others level 5, BUT the average ie most of the children would be a level 4! Now some 30 years on all children are expected to be at least level 4! Or is that because the Key Stage 2 SAT tests, especially in English, are so much simpler than when they began in the 1990s?

Many parents and children make the mistake of thinking that a choice of career is for secondary school and the children cannot make decisions at primary level. Actually as soon as the child enters secondary school, in my experience, they are set on to a moving timetable linked to exams and certain expectations of what they will become. Children need to be aware as young as possible of work opportunities around them – education for the real world – their world of work!

I was very aware that each child's social and emotional development was extremely important to the way they looked at life as they grew up. When asked where this was taught teachers said 'not in this subject but in science or literacy or PE lessons'. In fact it was taught in a myriad of different places. However, in order to ensure that crucial areas were taught we needed to formalise the subject.

I commissioned one of my part time teachers to see where in the curriculum we taught any aspect of Personal, Social, Moral or Health Education. Once finished it became a curriculum map which developed class by class. It was extremely interesting how much was taught implicitly in language lessons at Reception level, the stories used had moral content and involved many 'what would you do' scenarios! As time went on we included more and more into our map; Financial understanding became an explicit part of our entrepreneurial work in the two older classes and became a specific area for Work Experience at year 6.

I feel that our children were taught the very best moral values and did things for the right reasons. An example of their commitment to learning was shown quite clearly when a bright child joined our oldest class for her final year at junior school. In the library choosing reading books a discussion was heard between herself and another child-

New child: 'Why are you choosing such a thick book?'
Other child: 'Because it's interesting'
New child: 'But there's so much to read!'
Other child: 'Yes, but your book might be boring'

New child: 'But I can read it quickly'

Other child: 'But it might be boring'

This circular conversation went on for some time with each side having no understanding of where the other party was coming from!

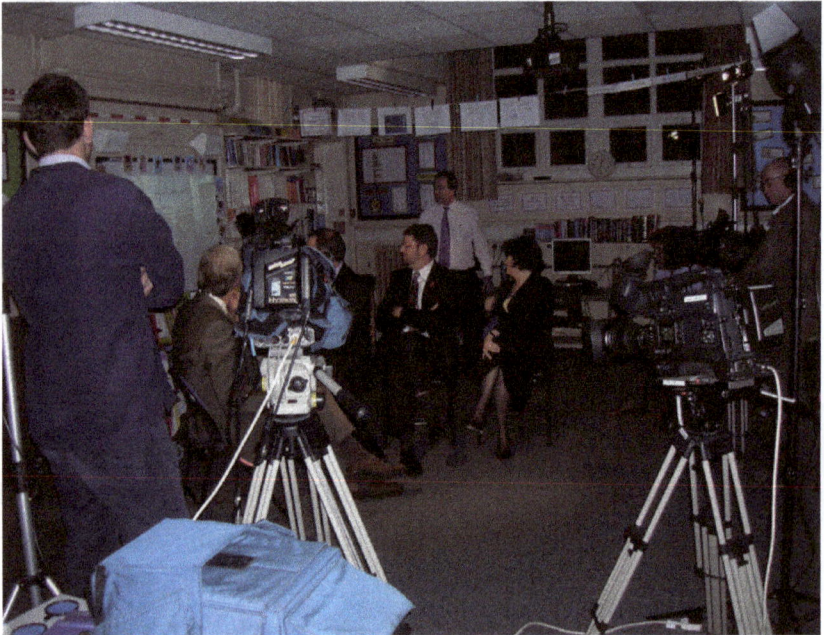

Recording 'A late night political programme for Anglia TV'. We worked with three local MPs, including Richard Bacon.

NOVEMBER 5TH 2005!!

"I know, I'll buy a firework box with a single lighter!! That will be safer all round!!"

Fireworks were bought annually to celebrate Guy Fawkes to the delight of the whole school with the added bonus of giving very practical teaching on Firework Safety! The previous year the teacher in charge of lighting the many fireworks had nearly burnt herself due to a smouldering firework bursting into life as another nearby was being lit. In the general excitement the children didn't seem to notice the lack of Firework Safety but the teachers did!!

Not wanting the children to go without I investigated further and found a cube box of fireworks which lit in a sequence once a single fuse had been lit.
'Oh yes', I thought – no problems this year!
Clutching two boxes I returned to school triumphantly.

The same teacher volunteered to be 'Firework Charlie' again and to save any problems we decided to keep the boxes apart but light both at the same time and retreat to a distance. What could go wrong?
Well quite a lot actually! The children came on to the playground excitedly; the firework boxes were placed 100 yards away on the adjoining playing field; Fuses lit 'Firework Charlie' walked quickly, but sensibly, back to join us. We watched in anticipation as the fuses burned red. THEN all hell let loose – fireworks leapt out of the

two boxes into the air letting off ear piercing bangs – the children retreated to the furthermost side of the playground! I have never known four minutes go past so slowly! Then with a sense of being in a echo chamber we all walked into school to sit quietly whilst our hearing returned.

Had they enjoyed the show?

The braver ones let out a resounding 'yes'; others holding their ears gave a more moderated response.

Then it began.

In came the secretary clutching mobile phone

'There's an irate villager on the phone for you Mrs Baldwin'.

And so it went on villager after villager followed by the chairman of the village council, who did seem to see the funny side of it all. Apologies were made, promises of never again; promises to read the box to see if all the fireworks were bangers, something I didn't think of; I was so pleased with my boxes! Apologies especially to the neighbour whose two dogs were terrified of fireworks and were being walked past the school early in the day to keep them calm for the evening – Oops!

THEN, horror of horrors! There were no sheep in the field opposite! I looked as far as I could whilst leaning out of the office window– sheep had definitely been peacefully grazing in the field adjoining the river that morning. Visions of carcasses of sheep, frightened to death by fireworks, floating down to Norwich drifted before my eyes, or even worse dying sheep aborting premature lambs!

I hastily sent two teaching assistants down the road to find the sheep - all was well, they may have been deafened by fireworks but they were grazing as if nothing had happened.

"ALL ONTO FATHER PATRICK!!"

Snowballs whistled past our ears - FP began manfully; throwing with gusto but wetness, cold, and an avalanche of snowballs beat him!!

"Two teams, top of the hill, five minutes to make an arsenal of snowballs! – GO!"

A rush for teams - then a race to the top of the hill for snowball making!

"READY STEADY GO!!"

A constant flurry of snowballs sailed from one team to the other. Hearts racing; faces red with excitement; hands blue with cold under the gloves; a bond of friendship and being 'in it together' exuded the hillside that morning!

Back to the minibus to change trousers; red knees; cold hands that couldn't find zips or buttons or laces .
The best morning ever!
Residential week is the greatest!

Residential Week was once a year for the older children. It was based across the country from Canterbury to Bath, Northumberland to York. The idea was to take the children out of their comfort zone, away from their mobile phones and constant communication with home, and to prepare them for life using their own, personal resources. Exploring their personal strengths and weaknesses. It certainly prepared them for the transfer to secondary school the next term.

Sometimes we self-catered and teams of children helped the adults cook and wash up. Sometimes we used a hostel where we ate with others and learnt how to choose meals, eat different food and mix socially with others.

In Bath we had Bath buns, the local Bath water and learnt to clap at the end of each piece of music played delightfully for us by a small group of musicians in the Pump Room.

In York we ran under the musical water fountains on the half hour.

In Northumberland we pretended to run out of fuel as we returned back across the causeway from Holy Island, just as the water was coming in!

And at every location, miraculously, the children met the ghost of Father Patrick during one of their nights!!

Residential week – hard at work in the kitchen!

Due to his tremendous involvement and dedication to the School Father Patrick's name was put forward by past and present governors to be included in the Queen's Honours List in 2008.

GRADUATE TRAINING PROGRAMME - GTP

When I retired I wanted to pursue three things;

I wanted to teach my Wednesday half day timetable for two terms as an unpaid volunteer until July 2009 to ensure my successor didn't have to worry about finding a replacement teacher with budgetary implications.

I also didn't want to disappoint the year 6 children, who would be looking forward to the Residential week and the Work experience week and I was fully prepared to volunteer to lead these as normal.

I also wanted to develop two areas of my career:

To build up our Nursery school so that it remained a first class Nursery

To further develop my GTP work and to become more involved in the programme.

I have always wanted to give something back to the profession that I loved so much.

As a member of the OSCITT schools we had been involved in providing a place for trainee teachers since

NEWSDESK (01603) 772443   Evening News, Thursday, April 10, 2003

Top of the class

School recognised for excellence in teacher training

by SIMON PARKIN
simon.parkin@archant.co.uk

A PRIMARY school in Norfolk has been recognised for its excellence in teacher training and gained an extra £45,000 a year in funding.

Bawburgh School has become the first primary in the county to be awarded teacher training status as part of a package of measures aimed at raising standards.

School Standards Minister David Miliband named the Hocking Lane school among an extra 50 schools being recognised for their excellence in providing Initial Teacher Training.

The school, one of just 46 Nationally Outstanding Primary Schools, will be given up to £45,000 worth of funding over the next four years to develop good teacher training practices in liaison with other schools in the city.

Headteacher Cindy Baldwin said the

DO YOU HAVE AN EDUCATION STORY FOR US?

Call education reporter Mark Moore on (01603) 772427 or e-mail him at mark.moore @archant .co.uk

recognition followed five years of being involved in developing teacher training in conjunction with Nottingham University.

"We have been helping schools with their work with new teachers on an informal basis, but we got no extra money despite it being a strain on resources," she said.

"We are absolutely delighted that this recognition and funding will allow us to properly co-ordinate it with other schools.

"We are already working on a trial teacher training model at Costessey High School."

Mrs Baldwin said the programme, which begins in September, will also allow Bawburgh to offer training packages to schools for the full range of classroom professions, from teaching to assistants.

"There are a lot of people who would like to work in a school but don't know how to go about it," she added.

The expansion of the training school programme, announced this week, brings the total number named Teaching Schools to 106 across England.

Notre Dame High School has joined Aylsham High School among the secondary schools to have gained the status and given extra annual funding of up to £56,000.

David Miliband said: "The new round of training schools will be an important addition to the overall strategy of improving teaching skills and raising classroom standards.

"Training Schools are at the cutting edge of training and developing teachers and make a real difference."

1997. We had a SCITT trainee every year from the OSCITT programme based at Nottingham University. We also gave Easter and summer term Teaching Practice experience to students from the University of East Anglia.

These experiences were vital to our school in many ways.

Firstly, each trainee was another pair of hands for our own class teachers, enabling smaller groups of pupils to be taught.

Secondly, it was very good for the teaching staff to see new ideas or ideas that one didn't think would work. But did! It was the trainee's enthusiasm that was catching whether they were with us for a year or six weeks!

Then, a few years later, another SCITT programme began in Norfolk and Suffolk. At first we were in competition for Norfolk trainees but later I really felt that the two could work alongside each other to our mutual benefit.

There were two programmes for trainees –
SCITT, school centred initial teacher training, for people with at least a 2.2 degree and who had some experience of working with children and wanted to become teachers in their own right. The SCITT programme was a very precise programme with clearly defined work elements each week. It looked at all aspects of teaching from the very basics upwards.
GTP, graduate training programme, for people again with at least a 2.2 degree but who had worked a great deal with children such as in schools as teaching assistants; people who worked in other capacities with children such as librarians. One of the most interesting applicants was from a zoo, she was in charge of children's groups! This was also a route in to teaching for people who had managerial experience and wanted a career change.

I became a SCITT and GTP mentor for both organisations. Our school awarded at least one place a year to a trainee.

I loved mentoring the GTP students. They had to work so hard to achieve the required standard of practise. The trainees were based over Norfolk and Suffolk: some visits were quite near but others demanded an early start and over an hour's drive in order to arrive before 9.00am and the start of the school day.

I found the journey to the schools easy but after a very exhausting day the journey back was very hard and concentration waned! So Fr. Patrick and Lorna would take me and pick me up at the end of the school day. This was a symbiotic relationship because I had a lift to the school and back, therefore, reducing the opportunity to crash on the way home! Fr. Patrick and Lorna had a day out wherever the school was – the coast was their favourite and could be reached from most of the schools. My mileage claim went to them when they drove so everyone was pleased.

I was made aware very soon that a venue for the whole of the GTP trainees was needed in Norfolk. As our hall had been recently completed and could hold that number of people I put it forward as a fortnightly training venue. This was accepted eagerly. The kitchen made it an ideal venue as meals could be provided for trainees which was good for them and gave the kitchen more 'paying guests'!

I became more involved in the organisation of the GTP programme and volunteered to do more work with them. At a committee meeting it was felt that the whole programme needed to be looked at as a year. This meant that all ends could be tied up; lecturers found and work given that was reflected in the lecture of the week. I volunteered to type up the year's programme, which was more difficult than it sounded! However, I did this for three years and it certainly helped the trainees and mentors keep ahead of the workload!

After retiring in 2008 I mentored five GTP trainees and felt that this part of my 'après retirement' plan was being fulfilled!

I was extremely delighted in June 2009 to be graded 'Outstanding' as a GTP mentor during a quality assurance review for the programme. This entailed being shadowed for the day by a senior mentor who looked at my approach with students; the developmental ideas given to the students and for my planning and records of the day.

At the same time I was approached to see if I would be interested in assessing Overseas teachers to give them full Qualified Teacher Status - QTS – in this country. I had retired by this time and I was delighted.
I had my training and my first assignment was allocated. I was to be mentored by a seasoned assessor to ensure that all went well. We were to meet at the school at 8.00am in three weeks' time on the Monday.

Geoff Robinson's letter to me on my retirement meant the world to me: a vindication of all my hard work and a promise of closer links with SNITT!

Suffolk & Norfolk Graduate Teacher Programme
Professional Development Centre
Woodside Road
Norwich
Norfolk NR7 9QL
Tel: 01603 433276 Fax: 01603 700236

Programme Leader: Geoff Robinson

Programme Administrators:
Debbie Barr, Bev Gregory and Rachel Strange
Email: debbie.barr@norfolk.gov.uk
beverley.gregory@norfolk.gov.uk
rachel.strange.edu@norfolk.gov.uk

SUFFOLK AND NORFOLK

GTP

ACCREDITED PROVIDER

Mrs C Baldwin
Headteacher
The Bawburgh School
Hockering Lane
Bawburgh
Norwich
NR9 3LR

8 December 2008

Dear Cindy

Congratulations on your 21 years at Bawburgh and on your retirement. I know that you will be greatly missed at the school but that Bawburgh will be in very good hands as Jan succeeds you.

I wanted to say on a personal level how much I have enjoyed working with you and to thank you for all that you have contributed to the GT Programme over the years. I hope that the association will continue into your 'retirement' and perhaps we can have a chat about that in the New Year when things are a little quieter for you.

In the meantime, I hope that you enjoy your celebration event on 19 December. Unfortunately, my diary commitments will not allow me to be there personally on the day but we are hoping that one of the GTP team will be there to represent us.

With all best wishes for your retirement, a very happy Christmas and a peaceful New Year.

Geoff Robinson

Suffolk County Council
Education

SNITT
www.snitt.co.uk

Norfolk County Council

THE CHILDREN GREW CONCERT BY CONCERT!

The Christmas concerts were full of agony and ecstasy!.
Each one began around August when I began to think of
a theme based on the Christmas story. Over the years I
looked at the story from all points of view; the
shepherds; the late Wise man; the lost sheep; The Magi.
Each year I would look at all the children in the school
and write the Christmas story that they would perform
for the parents.

Each year I found music and songs to accompany the
story. Sometimes our music teacher helped with the
songs and teaching the music to the orchestra and in
the latter years I taught the orchestra myself.
Actually they taught themselves! We knew the song and
the older children found the notes needed for each line.
The notes were put on the white board and we all tried
them out. Wrong notes were identified and somebody
would enlighten us as to what the correct note should
be!
It sounds chaotic but it was what Enterprise class did:
they knew the musical notes and now put them in the
correct order. It was noisy though!! BUT great fun!

Every child in the school had a part in the Christmas
concert. The youngest usually had an action song such as
'Twinkle Twinkle little Star' or a very simple song from

the play. They moved into position on the stage with the help of their older mentor in year 6 or 5 as part of the natural movement of the action.

As the children moved through the school they took on more and more acting or singing responsibilities! Year 1 or 2 children might be singing a solo or taking a major speaking part.
The concert afforded a platform for those whose talents were in performing in some way.

It was fascinating to watch the youngest children shyly sing their bit but also taking in how much the older children loved what the concert offered them. It was the high expectations of the school and the individual that gave children the courage to audition for major parts.
Year 6 children played most of the main parts but were tremendously supportive of younger children who were taking a lead somewhere in the play, they ensured that they were in the correct place and were ready to help with forgotten words or tunes. They clapped and congratulated with empathy!!

The orchestra practised with each different act and again supported each other. Slowing them down was my main worry and I constantly bellowed
'Listen to the choir!'
or alternatively
'Listen to the music!'
We usually worked with a musician who came and practised with us. The children were thrilled to be

working with an adult, who could really play an instrument well - sadly I couldn't! The orchestra were awed by the ease at which our pianists played and made great friends with them; which was very touching.

The live productions were a flurry of nerves; a once in a lifetime opportunity to do or die! AND they always performed above the expectations! It was so thrilling to watch them grow!

LOGOS!

When I arrived in 1987 we had a competition amongst the children to devise a logo for the school. It was to be used for our letter heading and all school uniform. One of our traveller children won with a circular picture which showed the school in all its Victorian glory - flower tubs et al.

In 1994 when the new classroom was added the oldest children worked together to produce an oval picture with an outline of the new school inside.

When the hall and kitchen were built, once again, the oldest children looked to review the logo. They decided to come up with something different and chose a photograph of the new school which included the school minibus parked on the playground. This was brilliant for the school letterhead but unfortunately the pixels were not enough for the uniform printers. It was unfortunate but we couldn't have two logos! The children and I spent several days worrying about what logo to have to show development. I didn't mention this to Fr. Patrick as in the great scheme of things it was way down the bottom of the list.

It was therefore absolutely amazing that on Wednesday he came in to school wafting a new logo. It had come to him in the night! It was gold and blue in colour, circular with a cross dissecting the circle into four triangular like spaces, the name of the school in the centre. Each triangular space held one word of TEAM - our mission statement:

The cross was in the centre of all of our work.

The children understood the philosophy behind the picture and thought it was brilliant. A Governors' meeting endorsed the logo which then went on to the minibus, the school letterhead and the school uniforms.

CELEBRATION of ACHIEVEMENT

What is achievement?
To me achievement is progress in *any* area of an individual's life. It can be academic; understanding of oneself and the consequences of one's actions; having greater empathy of others; physical development; or an area of the arts. But it can be seen by others as a positive change for the better.

At the end of each academic year we brought all these achievements together and awarded shields, cups, book vouchers to children of any age who had shown a discernible progress in some area of their development.

It's surprising but you remember most of the pupils you taught; you remember little stories about them, both funny and sad! You keep all those little, wonderful, warm private notes that are sent at the end of the year when they transfer to secondary school – 'they'll never forget you and will always come back to visit', and indeed many do and are warmly welcomed as 'helpers'!

Transfer to secondary school is very difficult for teachers as well. We remember the child that we saw at the age of four years old and gradually developed over seven years; their faults and achievements; their families.

In response to their need for continuity, and because we believed in what we were saying, every year six child who transferred from us was given a new Bible. We tried to give the same Bible that they had used in school and with which they were familiar.

The front piece was inscribed

This bible has been given to you from all of us at The Bawburgh School.
It is full of our love and thoughts as we wish you the very best for your future.
Please remember us.
We will always be here for you whenever you may need us .
Be there for us when we need you.

C.M.Baldwin Headmistress
Father Patrick Chair of Governors

We meant those words with all our hearts. The last line is quite poignant as it happened.
I wonder how many of you were there for us a few years later when we needed you?

PART FOUR

RETIREMENT

I wanted to make my retirement from the school as fluid as possible with no areas of concern for parents or staff. I wanted to express in my letter of resignation how much of my life the school had become and what a wrench leaving would mean to me. Therefore, I decided to announce my retirement date of December 31st 2008 at the Governors' meeting at the end of the Easter term in, retrospectively, quite an emotive way. The champagne was there, as were the tears, but the decision had been made – it was a decision I had made alone!

26/04/08

Dear Father Patrick,

I am writing to you, in your capacity as Chair of Governors, to formally inform you of my intention to resign as Headmistress of The Bawburgh School as from December 31st 2008.

I have enjoyed the position I have held here for the past 21 years immensely,

This school is my second home, I still get a thrill when opening the gates over a holiday or weekend and, looking at the picture in front of me, think 'this is mine'! However, I wish to retire whilst I am still 'good at what I do' and fit enough to actively enjoy my retirement years!

There is no better vocation than teaching. Each day is different or NFB (Normal for Bawburgh)! I envy newcomers to the profession, with their energy, enthusiasm and naivety of youth ready to conquer the world, even if during the bad times we all have to look on teaching as a 'job that brings in money'. However low the lows, they are more than made up for by the spiritual highs. Nothing could have given me greater job satisfaction than teaching, and teaching **here** at Bawburgh.

I would like to thank Governors, both past and present, for their consistent and unconditional support over these years. Particularly yourself, for being my 'critical friend' and working tirelessly with me to create a TEAM that has made The Bawburgh School the Outstanding centre of educational excellence that it is today.

I wish the school every success as it undoubtedly moves forward to greater things, my thoughts will **always** be here.

Yours faithfully

Cindy Baldwin

I urged the governors to appoint a replacement early in September so that I could work in tandem with whoever my replacement was to be for the Autumn term. Parents would be aware of my replacement and I would just slip away gradually.

I promised that, to help ease the new head teacher into the new year and to ensure that the year 6 children were able to have their Residential and Work Experience weeks, which they had looked forward to so much, I would organise them and lead them as normal. I also would be happy to keep my half day teaching until the end of the academic year to prevent having to employ another teacher before the following September.

I was going to be a teacher again, albeit for half a day and only for two terms BUT I wouldn't have any office or staffing responsibility, they would be taken up by my successor.

I would be free to help teach a class of children for an hour a week – JUST TEACH!!! It was what I wanted when I dreamed of being a teacher. The wheel had gone full circle!

This was the plan that didn't work –
It was also the first step on the road to disaster as you will read in the sequel 'Abuse of Power'!

21 YEARS

My lovely, supportive, governors took 'on board' what I had said.

I know that some people queried our, what they called 'Quest for awards' but what they didn't realise was that to win an award is not the goal at all. It is the developmental process involved moving towards that goal. It means that all staff are fully trained in an initiative that is only just beginning to come into schools. To be at the forefront means that everyone is fully conversant as to 'why' this particular initiative is being introduced into schools. It also ensures that everyone has been in at the beginning and helped with the changes. Understanding why things are changed helps staff to fully comprehend what the new initiative is about.

The governors wanted this innovative ethos to remain.

After interviews held in September my Deputy was appointed as my successor.
I took her off timetable for the Autumn term to give her the freedom to look at the school with new eyes. We had a whole term in which to inculcate her in the many nuances of 'heading up' a leading a school.

A TWENTY ONE YEAR TRIBUTE!

5th SEPTEMBER 2008

In celebration of my twenty one years' service the governors decided to take me out for a meal on the exact date that I had begun at the school all those years ago.

It was a local hotel and we looked over the past years with a certain nostalgia. We regaled those first dreadful pages that I had written in the school Log Book in 1987!! How the children couldn't draw a margin nor manage basic written work or basic computer literacy but were brilliant at using a BBC computer to move the cursor 'up' 'down' and 'shoot' to destroy robotic figures!

It was a great evening and even the few poor meals and my having food poisoning on the way home in no way diminished for me the delight in the recognition of having performed an excellent job!

21 Years On!

WARNING!

At my last Governors' meeting in December 2008 I pointed out that Children's Services did not like the way we ran our affairs. It did not seem to like being left out of our providers. We always used 'value for money 'providers: some of which were from the county but some from elsewhere.

It didn't like the fact that we had put self-made money into a high rate deposit account, with a higher interest rate than that offered by the county fund. Nor that we didn't pay into the County Building Fund because we made sure all of our building was regularly maintained and therefore, the fund wouldn't provide us with anything. We fully understood the concept that if all schools put a percentage of their annual budget into the Building Fund then there would be money for whatever school needed it most.

We didn't agree with this fundamental principle of schools that looked after their finances helping to fund other schools that didn't. A little like the benefits given to people who haven't saved for their retirement!

'NCC 'will want to bring the school back
into the fold, I warned.
Be prepared to support your new Head teacher'.'

A GOVERNOR CAME!

School life has to go on as usual even if it is the last few days of your career. One of the issues was to leave a strong Governing body. We had appointed a new parent governor and a new staff governor, both to take up their posts in January 2009. This would give my successor the opportunity to have some fresh faces. However, we also needed to consolidate the present governors who would be the leaders of the new team.

I felt that one of our Governors had become a little distant, a little disinterested in what we were doing. This governor had experience with committees, was very incisive and had no duplicity about him in any of his activities. I knew that he was upset I was retiring. Was he worried for the future? I thought the best thing to do was to ask him to come and see me and to talk things through face to face.

Next morning he arrived very 'perky' and I put to him my concerns. It appeared that it was work, his work that was taking its toll and nothing to do with us!

I asked the question that I had been mulling over for the past few weeks; would he consider putting his name forward to be considered for the role of Chair of Governors in the near future. I knew that Father Patrick was retiring at some point over the next term. He had expressed a desire to retire with me or even earlier at the end of the summer term 2008. However, he had been persuaded to stay on by my successor who had implored him to remain in place until she had settled into her new role. The governor seemed delighted to have been thought of and promised to think it over.

It had been so difficult to find somebody to take on the responsibilities of the Chair of Governors. A good Chairman has to know the school well and be really interested in what work it does and have a plan forged with the Head teacher, for the future. We had been incredibly lucky with Fr. Patrick who gave us a whole day a week and two weeks of his annual holiday for the benefit of the children. We were also lucky that Lorna, his wife, supported him and us so well. There's not many wives who would swop a week's holiday for a group of children tramping in and around their house for a week, come rain or shine, Nor to swop a second week of your annual holiday to live in a youth hostel room and help cook and look after fifteen year 5 and 6 children on a residential trip!

THE LAST DAY
FRIDAY DECEMBER 19TH 2008

The day had been planned well in advance.

I had been sent off the afternoon before whilst staff put up exhibitions of our achievements over the last twenty one years! The first half of the morning was a time for parents and previous pupils to visit the school and for me to catch up with everyone in an informal setting. The second half of the morning was my last school assembly shared with any parent or member of the community who wished to join us. Lunch was to be with the children and the last part of the afternoon Carol singing with parents and a final farewell! The late afternoon and early evening was a time for Governors, members of the local community and colleagues to enjoy. Our chef had been working on and off all week to produce a vast selection of snacks for the guests.

As I entered school that morning I had mixed emotions: I was absolutely drained, the obligatory end of term cold on its way. However, as usual the driven end of term adrenalin had kicked in and I could walk on water if I had to! Anyway I was looking forward to seeing former pupils and parents and rounding off my career in a positive way!

The day was a blur of meeting and greetings; the displays were brilliant allowing past pupils, friends and colleagues a smile of nostalgia as they saw themselves frozen in the past by photographs and features in magazines of school life. The press came out in force; local TV interviewed groups of children; the newspapers and local radio interviewed me – the obvious questions of how things have changed in education over the twenty one years. My answers leapt off my tongue easily –

'too much change too quickly has resulted in a lowering
of standards.
it takes a primary school seven years
to embed a new idea into a school,
constant changes mean children are confused and
basic teaching points are not really understood.
JUST LET TEACHERS TEACH!'

During the morning colleagues or their representatives from a wider field of education arrived and overwhelmed me with gifts and cards. Life was very good!

The children came into assembly singing 'Come My Lord' as they did every day and sat in their usual places. It was good to have a little bit of normality brought into the day! I had my children to talk to as a mother hen and her brood; the children were enthralled.

Towards the end of assembly there seemed to be a lot of quietly setting up of cameras, more women in black suits than I remembered before, a certain simmering of excitement. What happened next was unnervingly unreal! The Minister for Education, Mr Ed Balls, entered the hall with a magnificent bouquet of flowers which he proudly presented to me. Cameras rolled; we shook hands; microphones were pushed forward. He explained to the school that he had been a pupil many years ago when he was a small boy and his name was on the intake register! Hence the link! I must say he was very good with the children. He didn't talk down to them and asked specific questions – I was delighted that the children could think of why I was special and how I had helped them individually! Mr Balls rounded off his moment by exhorting everyone to give me three cheers with which, I whole heartedly joined in, by leaping to my feet at every cheer!

The children and Mr Balls watched as the Chair of governors and I planted a Magnolia tree which I had donated to the school and which I hoped would grow and flourish annually. The school had donated a plaque to stand in front of the tree as a permanent reminder of my time there.

It was perhaps unfortunate that the media asked similar questions again about developments in education over the past twenty one years whilst Mr Balls and I were together! I re-iterated my answers and Mr Balls gritted his teeth and smiled politely whilst muttering about me possibly looking back through rose coloured glasses, which, apparently you do as you get older!

As if it never happened the black cars were refilled with the important people; Mr Balls shook my hand for the last time and everyone drove off into the sunset.

I sent every child home with a personal Christmas card including a photograph and message just for them. I exhorted them to keep them safe in their memento box to read again in the future.

Parents didn't escape. My final letter to parents and the local community was as emotive as my resignation was to the governing body in an attempt to show them how far the school had come over the twenty one years – years before their children had even been thought of.

'Dear Parents and Friends,

When I arrived here in September 1987 the school was a very different place! The only rooms open for use were the present Enterprise classroom, the flat roof classroom and the present library which was the office. Mr. and Mrs. Clements, the caretakers, were absolutely wonderful & were never upset when we painted the background to our pictures actually on the display boards.

During my first year the class names, Enterprise, Endeavour, Satellites and Comets developed with different teaching approaches for each class. The present Comet classroom was opened up and the children entered school through the main blue door into a library area with sinks in! Gradually, over the years walls have been knocked down and girders put up to make the classroom what it is today. It was only very recently 2005 that it has been used for the youngest children prior to that it was always my classroom with Enterprise.

In 1989 we began to build up the creative subjects such as music and Scottish dancing – our Scottish teacher, Mrs Hunter, ensured that the haggis was piped in and 'addressed' correctly every year!

My beloved 'walk in cupboard' in the office had its wall removed, which gave us much more space and we began to look upstairs at the spider webbed, bedroom area. There were three rooms and we began by painting, as a whole staff of four, the back bedroom as an office. The office downstairs then became our staff room.

By the early 1990s we were beginning to link the school with local businesses and became the primary school representative on business/education link committees. We had begun to gain a reputation for 'thinking outside the box' and were being invited to join with other like minded people across the country to provide case studies for creative timetabling. Chris Woodhead was the Chief Inspector of schools at that time and we formed a great affinity with him.

He visited our school and was particularly interested in our use of specialist subject teachers, particularly in foreign languages.

An Outstanding Ofsted in 1996 was the basis for our involvement with Prince Charles and the Outstanding Primary Schools' Consortium. Together with other Head teachers I met with him at Highgrove House , a very exciting day, where he unveiled his plans for teacher training in 'fast moving schools' in which trainee teachers would learn from highly motivated staffs and develop a more charismatic attitude to teaching. Unfortunately, at the same time the government was introducing the Literacy hour, followed by the numeracy hour, all of which cut out creativity!

A general government crackdown on all subjects except, Maths, Literacy, ICT, Science and RE, gave us the drive to develop the creative subjects. ACE, Active Curriculum Enrichment, days began hence the termly voluntary contributions, which are essential for a creative curriculum. It was also the beginning of out World of Work programme, initiated by Father Patrick, who firmly believes that children need to know how work in school will prepare them for work in the real world when they leave school. Work Experience begins with the youngest children understanding jobs that people do in our school and culminates in Work Experience week for year 6 children when different types of work and working environments are visited.

At the same time we were putting in plans for a new classroom, pupils were spilling out of the three rooms! The school physically stopped at the end of the flat roof classroom corridor with a glass door leading straight on to the playing field. Outside toilets were still the order of the day in 1995!

The local authority would not fund a new classroom and so two grandparents of The Ragan family, who were builders, built the Ragan Room for us only charging the school for materials – probably there is an 'elf and safety' ruling now which would prevent this happening! At this moment the L.A. decided to upgrade our toilet block to indoor toilets. However, they insisted that the roofline of the toilet block followed the roof line of the original school, hence the classroom, although built earlier, has a roof line which doesn't match the existing one. Have a look!

We became a Primary Training School and linked with three secondary schools as the only Training schools in the East Anglian region. This involved bringing our work with Nottingham University, London and the S.E. together and made more sense of our role as a teacher training centre. As you know from the many cars on the playground on some Thursdays we are still heavily involved in teacher training and organise the Core Training programme for the Norfolk and Suffolk trainee teachers. This greatly enhances the curriculum that we can give the children as we have to be in at the forefront of new ideas.

Yet again we needed more office space and the second bedroom was made into an office for me. However, this didn't last long as the wall between the two offices came down to create one large space in which Mrs Knights, the secretary could really spread out. However, in 2002 bedroom 3 became my Head teacher's room, the place children shouldn't like coming to but they love popping into see me. I think they want to see if I'm still there!!

In 1998 we opened our own kitchen where the present staff

room is now and the numbers of children eating a hot lunch rose from seven to approximately fifteen! However, two cooks later we found a chef in Clive! School meals have risen to an average of 35 a day. This coupled with Over 60's luncheons; Class parent lunches; GTP lunches; Take Outs; Tuck shop; Birthday Tables have all helped to make the kitchen a success.

With the Southern Bypass opening I was always worried that houses would be built beyond the Bypass and the school wouldn't be able to cope with the extra numbers. When the agricultural field behind school became available we submitted an application for grant funding which we could fund match by selling our smaller field, prime building land, to finance a much needed hall and kitchen. The concept of our own hall began in 1988 but we were constantly thwarted; In 1993 the Governors even chose the windows of our new hall but it all fell through at the last meeting! After four years our hall, kitchen, nature area and large playing field was a reality.

Over these 21 years I have a wealth of wonderful memories, notably of the children, who are absolutely fantastic: the children working with the London Symphony Orchestra to write and play the 'Fanfare' for the Norfolk and Norwich Festival at St. Andrews Hall; Residential trips; Freezing outside Norwich Cathedral waiting with the children to perform a dance/drama for the 500th anniversary! The cheers and looks on the children's faces when we drove our first minibus into school; The invite to the Queen's Garden Party with Father Patrick for our services to Education; My funniest memory is of my first day here when a Mum called to say that Pamela was stuck in France and wouldn't be attending that day, we were a little puzzled as we couldn't find her on the register but that was the least of our problems and quickly forgotten. At the same time I was wondering where our secretary Pam Knights was. Only in the afternoon did I put two and two together and realise that my Pam Knights and little Pamela were one and the same!

I will always remember the children and the school that has been my life for so long. I hope that it will give your children and you as much pleasure in the future.
Yours faithfully

C. M. Baldwin'

Parents and children left quickly vanishing into the dark shadows of winter. I changed into a long dress for the after school part of the day, I looked old and haggard I thought as I regarded myself in the mirror – one last part to play!

I relaxed, enjoying seeing old friends and colleagues. We laughed together at shared anecdotes and tried to remember dates and years as we looked at the displays.

During the early part of the evening we watched the local news and 'yes' there I was jumping up and down to the three cheers of my children. My husband did point out rather loudly that I was not supposed to cheer myself! I also heard myself decrying the education of today and the lowering of standards.

Thanks, Mr Balls

BLAST FROM THE HEAD

MAKING a visit to the primary school that set him on the path to becoming an MP should have been an opportunity for positive spin.

Ed Balls presented head Cindy Baldwin with flowers to mark her retirement from Bawburgh School near Norwich, in Norfolk, after 21 years and thanked her for being a 'brilliant teacher'.

Unfortunately Mrs Baldwin was less than complimentary about him – or at least his accomplishments as Children's Minister.

Speaking to journalists after his visit, the teacher said: 'The whole state of education is going down hill rapidly. The idea of education, education, education has totally slipped.'

s.doughty@dailymail.co.uk

Daily Express Monday December 22 2008   15

By Sara Dixon

Six of the best for Balls over crisis in schools

CHILDREN'S Secretary Ed Balls went back to his old school and was given a lesson in how to run the country's education system.

The Education Minister – who was recently forced to issue an apology over this summer's SATs fiasco – paid a surprise visit to his former primary school.

But instead of going to the top of the class, the 41-year-old minister was given a dressing-down by the school's current head over the state of Britain's education system.

Cindy Baldwin, who is retiring after 21 years at Bawburgh School near Norwich, left the school's old boy under no illusions about what she thought of the dire situation in the nation's schools.

The head of the 85-pupil school told Mr Balls that the quality of children's education is suffering under Labour's directives.

Mrs Baldwin said: "The whole state of education is going down hill rapidly. The idea of Education, Education, Education has totally slipped."

Forced

She criticised the push for breakfast clubs and after-school clubs and attacked the Government for encouraging a culture where parents are forced to work. It meant no one was at home to look after their children.

She added: "In a time when there are fewer jobs, why send people out to work?

"It would be better to pay people to be at home to look after their children."

Mrs Baldwin also criticised repeated launches of new initiatives that took seven years to implement but were superseded

Mrs Baldwin and Balls at his old school. Top, his name in the register

Picture: ADRIAN JUDD

Young Ed is well mannered, but he must try harder

The children's secretary, Ed Balls, visited his old primary school last week, only to be told by the head teacher that his work isn't up to scratch. Cindy Baldwin, who is retiring after 21 years, made it plain that she's not impressed by Labour's record on education.

"The whole state of education is going downhill rapidly," she said — a little ungratefully, you might think — after Balls presented her with flowers. "The idea of education, education, education has totally slipped."

She complained (like many teachers) about new initiatives that took seven years to implement, only to be replaced by other initiatives after two years.

And how did Balls respond to this scathing report card? "It feels very strange to be back here after 33 years," he said.

At home I read the Farewell card from my successor.

ever take away your achievements of the past 21 years. I love the school as much as you do and I promise to look after it carefully and thoughtfully. You will be a very hard act to follow, but I'll try!

Thank you, oh wise one. A truly outstanding head.

All my love, on this your last day as head!

Jan
x

19/12/08

Dear Cindy,

So, how do you thank someone who has had such an impact on your life? I can still clearly re-call the day we met — little did I know what lay in store (?

I have loved working with you — so many highs, so much fun and laughter, so many challenges. You have been many things over the years: friend, colleague, mentor and coach. I know that I would not be the person that I am today if you hadn't been the leader that you are — you have given me the opportunity to grow and develop, and you have been there to poke and prod me out of my comfort zone.

I know how hard the last weeks have been for you, but nothing can

How touching, truthful and thoughtful I thought!

132

I looked back over the past 21 years.

Could I have done more?

Could I have done better?

No!

I had worked as hard as I could. I was handing over:

- A school beautifully furbished;

- The nicest hall and kitchen that I had ever seen in any school:

- Two fully paid for minibuses, one only a term old:

- A Governors' fund with £62,000 in – ample to pay off the overdraft - if the school was forced to before the new April budget arrived;

- Plans for a large conservatory and new drains at the back of the school had been paid for and awaited a date for completion.

- A grant for a Nursery building to be built on site applied for – although it had to be applied for by a nursery once built it would become the property of the school.

- A lovely, supportive staff with a wide range of interests and teaching approaches.

My husband and I left for Hong Kong early the next morning for a two week holiday – for me it was to break the mould of school and to return refreshed to begin a new life. We thoroughly enjoyed our holiday not realising the media frenzy back home of Mr Balls visit to school and my views on the lowering of educational standards.

THE SEQUEL - ABUSE of POWER

Cindy Baldwin & Father Patrick Kerley

CHAPTER 1
Return

The first Wednesdays of the New Year were magic – I had no head teacher responsibilities – I was able to just enjoy my day with the children as a voluntary helper!

On the first three Wednesdays of the new term I arrived at school and checked over the minibus. All the children were in class and I waited patiently for them to line up and file onto the minibus ready to go swimming. Father Patrick would drive the new minibus onto the playground and pick up his quota of children. I was so proud as we pulled out of the school gates one behind the other with the school name emblazoned on the sides of the minibuses.

It felt very good to be a bus driver with no other responsibilities!

Father Patrick and his wife Lorna

Telling a Lie

What does telling a lie actually do to your soul?

Are 'white lies' a lesser scale? 'Does my bum look big in this?' would normally elicit a quick 'No' in 99% of cases I would think! A 'white lie'?

What about the bigger, premeditated rehearsed lies, the type that cause unnecessary pain. The type that cause uncalled for humiliation? What do they do to your inner being, your very soul?

A lie leads inexplicably to another and another. The devil ensures that there is no way back. You are accompanied; then pushed; then dragged along the road of no return.
Can you see the devastation the first lie caused?
Does it please you?
When does the full horror of what you have unleashed make itself known? When you realise how your first lie has been used by other forces for evil? When you realise you were used by a greater evil?

Do you ever accept your guilt or do you bury your head and believe your lie?
Do you feel vindicated as the lie grows and circulates, embellished as it grows, sending seeds of untruths into the community at large?

What about those on the other end of the lie? The

receiving end? What do they do?

We believe as Christians that we shouldn't retaliate. The temptation is great. The devil is powerful. He started the lie in the first place!

When you die what happens to your soul?

Without our faith I'm not sure that one of us or both of us would have committed suicide.
Everything we had built up had gone.
Social networking ensured that playground gossip, quite untrue and unfounded, was circulated far and wide from past pupils at universities to pupils in secondary schools. Some parents seemed to revel in the salacious gossip. Those that knew us and our work knew better!

Father Patrick and I believe that God has a plan for all of us.

I re-iterate a previous question,
Where was God in all of this?
Was he with us, suffering with us in the midst of our distress?

We believe he is always with us, in our suffering, our disappointments, in our heartbreaks.
We both called on him in our different ways.
We found help!
Strength to fight!
Strength to go on!

However, I doubt if anyone could have dreamt of what was about to unfold!

BETRAYAL

SATURDAY JANUARY 24th 2009

'Saturday morning began damp and became full and stormy as the morning progressed with wind blasting in all directions; rain coming down like stair rods; dank darkness promising a long Winter.

Lorna and I had twice battled across the market at Great Yarmouth carrying a potato sack each, piled high with vegetables for our school kitchen. The clothes hung on us. Huge freezing globules of rain ran down our necks as we sat in a freshly steamed up car, breathing the interesting fumes of wet cabbages!

The last lap of this, our normal Saturday routine, was to drive to school and fill up the fridge ready for the next week of school meals. Today, as we warmed up, the car became unpleasantly hot and sticky.

The post was on the mat as usual when we got home. I opened, with interest, the brown envelope from Children's Services that was to change my life irrevocably.'

Fr. Patrick